SYRACUSE UNIVERSITY   12460260
Profits in the modern economy ...
HB 601.C572 1964

3 2911 00020605 2

HARVEY M. RICE

HENRY FORD II

RICHARD H. HOLTON

LEIF H. OLSEN

DEXTER M. KEEZER

EDMUND A. MENNIS

FREDERICK L. DEMING

MYRON J. GORDON

CARL L. NELSON

PEARSON HUNT

HOWARD G. SCHALLER

JOEL SEGALL

DIRAN BODENHORN

FRANCIS M. BODDY

HAROLD BIERMAN, Jr.

J. FRED WESTON

ROBERT K. JAEDICKE

ROBERT W. JOHNSON

DANIEL M. HOLLAND

WALTER W. HELLER

PROFITS
IN THE
MODERN
ECONOMY + + +

*Selected Papers from
a) Conference on
Understanding Profits,* Macalester College and
University of Minnesota, 1964,

edited by
HAROLD W. STEVENSON
and J. RUSSELL NELSON

*University of Minnesota Press
Minneapolis*

© Copyright 1967 by the University of Minnesota. All rights reserved

Printed in the United States of America at the
North Central Publishing Company, St. Paul

Library of Congress Catalog Card Number: 67-13120

PUBLISHED IN GREAT BRITAIN, INDIA, AND PAKISTAN BY THE OXFORD
UNIVERSITY PRESS, LONDON, BOMBAY, AND KARACHI, AND IN CANADA
BY THE COPP CLARK PUBLISHING CO. LIMITED, TORONTO

The paper by Diran Bodenhorn, "A Cash-Flow Concept of Profit," is
reprinted, with permission, from the *Journal of Finance*, XIX (March
1964), 16–31, copyright 1964 by the American Finance Association. The
Certainty Model on p. 140 has been adapted by J. Fred Weston, with permission, from M. H. Miller and F. Modigliani, "Dividend Policy, Growth,
and the Valuation of Shares," *Journal of Business*, XXXIV (October
1961), 423, published by the University of Chicago Press, copyright 1961
by the University of Chicago.

HB/
60/
CP72
196Xaa

HB
601
C572
1964

List of Sponsors

THIS volume is based upon papers presented at a Conference on Understanding Profits held at Macalester College and the University of Minnesota on April 22–24, 1964. Co-chairmen of the conference were Paul V. Grambsch, Dean, School of Business Administration, University of Minnesota, and Arthur R. Upgren, now retired, Frederick R. Bigelow Professor of Economics and Director of the Bureau of Economic Studies, Macalester College.

Members of the Sponsoring Committee were Elmer L. Andersen, former Governor of Minnesota, H. B. Fuller Co.; Julian Baird, Chairman of the Board (ret.), First National Bank of St. Paul; Bjorn Bjornson, Information Manager, Northern States Power Co.; Herbert P. Buetow, Chairman of the Finance Committee, Minnesota Mining & Manufacturing Co.; John Carroll, President, American Hoist & Derrick Co.; E. A. Cashin, Chairman of the Board, Naegele Outdoor Advertising Co. of Minnesota, Inc.; Grady Clark, then President, Investors Diversified Services, Inc.; George D. Dayton II, Executive Vice-President, The Dayton Co.; Benjamin J. Greer, Director, The Pillsbury Co.; A. B. Jackson, Chairman of the Board, St. Paul Fire & Marine Insurance Co.; Lester A. Malkerson, President, Malkerson Motors, Inc.; Otto A. Silha, Vice-President, Minneapolis Star and Tribune; F. K. Weyerhaeuser, Chairman of the Board, Weyerhaeuser Co.; Wheelock Whitney, Chairman of the Board, J. M. Dain & Co., Inc.; Charles J. Winton, Jr., Co-Chairman of the Board, The Winton Co.

The following sponsoring organizations and persons were among those that contributed money to make the conference possible:

Profits in the Modern Economy

American Hoist & Derrick Foundation

Elmer L. & Eleanor J. Andersen Foundation

The Andreas Foundation

Batten, Barton, Durstine, & Osborne, Inc.

The F. R. Bigelow Foundation

Patrick Butler Family Foundation

Cargill, Inc.

Leonard G. Carpenter

J. M. Dain & Co., Inc. Foundation

George D. Dayton II

Edwin S. Elwell

Foley Brothers, Inc.

General Mills, Inc.

Great Northern Railway Co.

Benjamin G. Griggs

Louis W. and Maud Hill Family Foundation

Geo. A. Hormel & Co.

Stanley Hubbard Foundation, Inc.

International Milling Co., Inc.

Al Johnson Construction Co.

Lampert Lumber Co.

George P. Leonard

Minnesota & Ontario Paper Co.

Minneapolis-Moline, Inc.

Minneapolis Star & Tribune Fund

Minnesota Mining & Manufacturing Co.

Munsingwear, Inc.

Northern States Power Co.

Northwestern Bell Telephone Co.

Northwest Paper Foundation

Peavey Co. Group Foundation

George S. Pillsbury

The Pillsbury Co.

John R. Stoltze

United States Steel Corp.

Waco Foundation

Waldorf Paper Products Co.

Webb Foundation, Inc.

Wheelock Whitney Foundation

Winton Fund

Martin Wunderlich Foundation

Foreword

FINANCIAL profit and the profit motive are strangely misunderstood in our society by many persons you would think should understand them. For a number of years both financial profit and the profit motive have been on the defensive in many parts of the world. There does appear now to be some change in this attitude, in some quarters at least, and we hope that we can help to further this trend through this book. The reasons for the misunderstanding are many. The spread of education among hundreds of millions of people makes it possible for them to learn what is happening throughout the world. The spread of newspapers, radio, and television instantly brings information from worldwide sources to the most remote villages of Siberia and Africa. But increased knowledge of the vast chasm between the material welfare of the countries with a capitalist economy on the one hand and the countries with socialist, communist, or undeveloped economies on the other hand has produced more envy, jealousy, and hatred. The have-nots do not interpret their position to be the result of lack of raw material, motivation, or technology, or the lack of capital and know-how — rather, they attribute their position to be the result of selfish, greedy profit-making by those of whom they are envious.

In our own culture there are also many who mistakenly reach the same conclusion and who take profit as somehow unethical, immoral, and sinful. Yet, without the profits that have been produced by the capitalist economies of the world, man would still be living in a civilization of poverty, hand production, miserable existence plagued by widespread illness, health-breaking toil, and a hopeless future. Surely we need a better understanding of profits and all the ramifications of the profit system.

What has been happening to financial profits in our economy within recent years? Most significantly, almost nothing has been happening. Profits have not increased even during the years in which our gross national product has doubled. Net profits in the 1950's averaged about $22 billion a year. So far in the 1960's, in spite of the tremendous rise in our production, they have averaged almost the same amount. At the same time, the wage portion of the gross national product has doubled as the gross national product has doubled. Profits have not been great enough to buy all of the new, highly productive machinery needed to keep raising the wage values of our output. New money will not enter this phase of our economy when all curves are upward except the profit curve, which remains flat.

It also takes profit to provide additional capital to create new jobs for people in addition to those performed by machines. It takes profit to pay taxes — to maintain state universities, for example. It takes profit to make financially possible a non-tax-supported college. Hence, Macalester College is an integral part of the free-enterprise system of profits. We continue to remain in business here only so long as we sell our services, education, at a quality high enough to attract purchasers and investors and with sufficient business efficiency to operate our competitive enterprise in the black. We, therefore, believe in the free-enterprise, capitalist system. We are glad to be able to help spread knowledge and information about the profit of that system.

Editors' Preface

PROFITS are generally acknowledged by thoughtful citizens to be essential to the workings of a private, free-enterprise economy. The careers of some people are closely associated with the investment decisions of business organizations in striving toward goals of profit. The lives of many other people are affected by the profit experience of corporations. Still others are concerned with theoretical aspects of profits and with the influences of profits upon the American economy.

Unfortunately, there is no general agreement about the term "corporate profits," and this has led to less than satisfactory communications between people with seemingly different opinions on the subject of profits. In particular, the matters of what constitutes "profit," how profit should be measured, and how profit contributes toward a healthy, vigorous economy lead to frequent disagreement or confusion.

It is not surprising for different people analyzing the same array of financial figures to come up with different interpretations. These differences may arise simply because the people apply different values to the data or bring different insights into their interpretations. In the matter of corporate profits, the same financial data used by different people give rise to different determinations of profit. Some determinations differ very little, and the consequences from their use are not serious, but some interpretations differ widely. The various uses to which profit data are put and the various definitions of corporate profits to meet particular needs or to foster certain impressions have not brought better communications about profits. Therefore, the public has many misconceptions about profits.

Profits in the Modern Economy

One example of the problem of communication is the economist's and the accountant's differing concern for the future and the past in their attention to profits. Likewise, the business manager and the labor official quite obviously emphasize interpretations of profits best representing their interests. Academicians differ among themselves about theoretical concepts of profits and the process of decision-making. The term "profits" can also be used by any of these people in respect both to a single firm and to the aggregate of many firms.

As a means of focusing upon the various shadings in meanings in the use of the term "corporate profits," a Conference on Understanding Profits was held April 22–24, 1964, at Macalester College and at the University of Minnesota. The conference was conceived by Arthur R. Upgren and sponsored jointly with Paul V. Grambsch as a setting in which leaders in business, government, and education would air their views on corporate profits for the enlightenment of all. The fact that the audience actually comprised leaders of business, labor, and government as well as academicians further indicates the task of achieving general understanding and interest faced by the speakers.

Some twelve years earlier, a similar purpose was served successfully in a Conference on Savings, Inflation, and Economic Progress held at the University of Minnesota. The published proceedings, *Savings in the Modern Economy* (University of Minnesota Press, 1953), represented a notable addition to the literature on the savings process. The three editors of that earlier volume, Walter W. Heller, Francis M. Boddy, and Carl L. Nelson, also participated in the April 1964 conference on profits.

Publication of selected papers from the conference on profits in this volume provides the serious reader with a comprehensive discussion of the current beliefs about the role of profits in an economy. Enlightenment about differing viewpoints can lead to better understanding, which, in turn, will be a framework for clearer thinking about corporate profits.

The conference was made possible by a generous donation from the Louis W. and Maud Hill Family Foundation as well as by contributions from business firms and individual donors from the Minneapolis–St. Paul area. The names of the sponsoring committee and of the larger donors are given in the List of Sponsors.

Conference planners from Macalester College were Arthur R. Upgren, Lloyd Buckwell, and James Weekly and from the University of Minnesota were Paul V. Grambsch, J. Russell Nelson, and Harold W. Stevenson. Executive director of the conference was Major General John S. Guthrie, U.S. Army (Ret.).

In the time between the Conference and the publication of this book, several men have changed their positions: Arthur R. Upgren retired from Macalester College and is now professor emeritus; Edmund A. Mennis shifted from the Wellington Management Company, Philadelphia, to the Republic National Bank of Dallas; Richard H. Holton moved from the Department of Commerce to the University of California, Berkeley; Walter W. Heller returned to the University of Minnesota from his chairmanship of the Council of Economic Advisers; Howard G. Schaller moved from Tulane University to Indiana University; and Frederick L. Deming of the Federal Reserve Bank of Minneapolis was named Under Secretary of the Treasury, Monetary Affairs.

The assistance of the speakers at the conference in the further tasks of preparing their papers for this volume is very greatly appreciated. In certain papers pertinent data have been brought up to 1966; the editors are particularly indebted to Walter W. Heller for his efforts to provide a 1966 perspective on the outlook for profits. The guidance and care exhibited by Anne Harbour Jirasek of the University of Minnesota Press in the preparation of the book is warmly appreciated.

HAROLD W. STEVENSON
J. RUSSELL NELSON

Minneapolis
September 1966

Table of Contents

PROFITS IN THE FIRM

PROFITS AND NATIONAL ECONOMIC POLICY

THE PROBLEM
AND ITS SETTING + + +

Editors' Introduction

PROFIT is a concept about which there is much misunderstanding. The man in the street, the businessman, and the economist all think of profit in different senses and for this reason experience difficulty in communicating with each other. Even among persons who think they have agreed on definitions, discussion often flounders in ambiguity because the term is being used to convey various shades of meaning.

The meanings attributed to the word "profit" range from the view that it is the entire return received by the businessman to the view that "pure" profit is the residual after deductions from total income for wages, interest, and rent. This latter view has evolved from attempts to explain the source of profit. These attempts have developed along two lines. J. B. Clark argued that profit results exclusively from dynamic change, e.g., inventions, which yield temporary profit to entrepreneurs. F. B. Hawley held that risk bearing is the essential function of the entrepreneur and is the basis for profit. While differing on many points, proponents of both these views regard profit as a residual.

Further confusion about the term "profit" arises from its use in reference to a single firm, in reference to the aggregate of all firms, or as an element of national income. Often the term "profit" is used to represent both an amount in dollars of residual income and a percentage of return on invested capital or sales. Thus, when a representative of business, labor, or government is discussing profit, he is likely to select the usage which best supports his point of view.

The essay by Henry Ford II illustrates these difficulties. In it he presents statements from a wide variety of sources which assert that profits are high, or rising, and he then seeks to demonstrate that real profits have declined during much of the postwar period. While not a work of scholarship, Ford's paper is a thoughtful statement by a leading businessman that focuses attention on some of the thorny issues in the study of profit.

How High Is Up?

As EVERYONE who has ever reared children knows, the simplest questions are sometimes the hardest to answer. For example, How high is up? I ask you to consider a question just as simple to ask and just as hard to answer: How high are profits?

The news is full of answers, and all of them seem to run in the same direction: Profits at record high, say the headlines. Profits up 52 per cent, say the President's economic advisers. Profits are staggering, says Walter Reuther. The profit squeeze is over, says *Time*. These are all, in their fashion, answers to my question. Let us consider them.

It is, of course, true that the total dollar volume of profits was higher in 1963 than ever before. Corporate after-tax earnings for 1963 are estimated at $27 billion — 11 per cent above the previous high. But many other economic records were also set in 1963. Gross national product, personal income, labor force, employment, taxes, industrial output — all were higher than ever before. There is, therefore, no special significance about the fact that profits, too, were higher. Indeed, it would be startling if they were not.

Nor should it be considered remarkable that profits were up 52 per cent, in view of the fact that the measurement was taken from the bottom of the previous recession to the highest point reached after three years of strong recovery. Profits were up even more — over 60 per cent — in less than half this time during the preceding recovery period.

NOTE: Reprinted by permission of the Ford Motor Company. Delivered at the 12th Annual Management Conference of the University of Chicago, March 5, 1964.

Profits in the Modern Economy

The fact that Walter Reuther is staggered isn't very significant either. Mr. Reuther is always staggered by profits in the automobile industry, especially in a negotiation year — even, as I remember, in 1958, when many of us in the industry were staggered by our lack of profits.

The conclusion that the profit squeeze is over would seem to mean that profits are now high enough or back to normal. But, if this is the meaning, then we have to ask, How high is enough? and What is normal? Since these questions are even harder to answer than mine, I propose that we put them aside for the moment and go back to the relatively simple question, How high are profits?

One answer, as I have said, is that profits in 1963 amounted to $27 billion. Now, the trouble with $27 billion is that it has too many zeros. Nobody has a reliable, instinctive feel for the size of anything that's measured by an eleven-digit number.

Perhaps we can begin to get a feel for the size of profits by comparing them with some other things. For example, total corporate sales in 1963 were in the neighborhood of a trillion dollars. A little arithmetic tells us that corporate profits were, therefore, about 2.7 cents per dollar of sales. In other words, corporations, on the average, incurred expenses of 97.3 cents to earn 2.7 cents.

There are various other economic measures that we might compare with corporate profits. Corporate profits represent about four and a half cents for each dollar of gross national product, about six cents for each dollar of personal income, and about thirteen cents for each dollar of compensation to corporate employees. Corporate profits about equal the increase in employee compensation that occurs every eighteen months in our rapidly growing economy. Corporate profits also about equal the total tax collections for social security and unemployment insurance. Corporate after-tax profits are less than half the total amount of taxes collected from or through corporations.

At this point, we have two sets of answers to the question, How big are profits? The first set suggests that profits are very, very big. The second set suggests that profits aren't really so big after all. Taken together, they suggest that the answer depends entirely on what one compares profits with. As a matter of fact, How high are profits? is about as useful a question as How high is up? To get useful answers, we really have to change the question. One possible substitute is this: Are corporate profits bigger or smaller than they used to be, relative to other things they might reasonably be compared with? In other words, Are profits growing as fast as other factors in the economy?

This question produces some answers that make sense, for most of the possible answers point in the same direction. Almost everything is growing faster than profits, and profits, therefore, are smaller relative to almost everything else than they used to be.

First, How fast are profits growing? After-tax profits, $27 billion in 1963, were $23.5 billion in 1956, nearly $23 billion in 1950, and more than $20 billion as long ago as 1948.

Since 1950, profits have risen $4.4 billion, or less than 20 per cent. Meanwhile, here is what has happened to other factors in the economy: gross national product, up 106 per cent; employee compensation, up 120 per cent; weekly wages in manufacturing, up 70 per cent; business investment in new plant and equipment, up 90 per cent; per capita disposable personal income, up 56 per cent; government spending — federal, state, and local — up 179 per cent; prices, up 33 per cent.

Let me repeat that last figure: since 1950, prices have gone up 33 per cent. This, of course, means that a substantial part of the dollar increases in the other categories resulted from inflation rather than from any real gain. This is true of each of these categories, but I call special attention to the fact that corporate profit is the only item on the list that has gone up *less* than prices. This, in turn, leads us to the startling conclusion that since 1950 profits have really gone down, rather than up. When the record-breaking profits of 1963 are converted to 1950 dollars, they shrink from $27 billion to $20.5 billion — 10 per cent below the actual profits of American corporations in 1950.

In short, when we measure our national economic performance in constant dollars, we find that 1963 was not the year of highest profits for American corporations. That record belongs to 1950. And 1963 was not even the second-best year — 1948 takes second place, with 1963 in third, a nose ahead of 1955 and 1956.

In relative terms, of course, profits have suffered a sharp decline. Consider, for example, the relation between profit and sales. In the five years beginning in 1950, corporate profits averaged 3.6 per cent of sales. During the next five years, 1955–1959, the profit margin was down to 3.1 per cent — a decline of 14 per cent. During the first three years of the 1960's, the margin averaged only 2.6 per cent — a further decline of 16 per cent.

Profits in the Modern Economy

When we consider profits as return on investment, we get similar results. In the five years 1955–1959, the profits of manufacturing corporations averaged 11.4 per cent of stockholder equity. During the first three years of the 1960's, the return averaged only 9.4 per cent — a decline of 18 per cent.

How high are profits? By any relative measure, profits are now at about the same level as they were during the 1954 recession. In 1964, after three full years of rising prosperity for the rest of the economy, profits have finally climbed back up until they are as high as they were at their lowest point in the decade after the end of World War II.

If it is true that profits were record-breaking in 1963, then the record was a new low — not a new high. In the postwar era, profits have never been so low at a high point in the business cycle as they are today. The trend is plain: corporate profits amounted to 8 per cent of gross national product in 1950, 5.8 per cent in 1955, 5.1 per cent in 1959, and 4.7 per cent in 1963.

At this point, I think we can best continue our inquiry into the size of profits by once again changing our question. Even though profits are steadily shrinking, there are many people who seem to believe that profits are as high as, or even higher than, they ought to be. How high should profits be? How do we know?

It seems to me that there are two approaches to this problem. One is the modern-day version of the Robin Hood approach, which assumes that the way to make people better off is to spread the existing store of wealth. Applied to the corporation, the Robin Hood approach leads to the conclusion that corporations can always afford to keep less of their income and give others more. Since most corporations make far more money than most individuals, this conclusion has a great deal of superficial plausibility about it. It also has a strong emotional appeal, as the popularity of the Robin Hood legend and of variations on it over the centuries testifies.

The trouble with this approach is that it can't possibly do very much for many people very long. Even if one ignored all the side effects that would result from redistributing present profits, the profits just aren't big enough to go very far. Corporate profits are only about the size of one year's increase in gross national product. In other words, each year the growth of the economy provides as much new wealth for the American people as the total amount of corporate profits. This suggests that the American people have much more to gain from the continuing growth of the economy than they could possibly gain by dividing up the profits of corporations.

This also suggests a second approach to the problem of deciding how high profits should be. This approach begins by inquiring into the relation between profits and growth. What happens to the growth of the economy when the rate of profit goes down, as it has in recent years? What would happen if we could do something to bring profits back up again?

The relation among business, profit, and economic growth is basically very simple. Profit determines investment, and investment is essential to growth. Thus, a steep and continuing decline in profit is likely to mean a serious drop in investment and, therefore, slower growth for the economy. In these circumstances, higher profit would mean higher investment and faster growth.

The decline in profits during the postwar period has in fact been accompanied by a sharp decline in business investment. Business expenditures for new plant and equipment averaged 7.9 per cent of gross national product from 1947 through 1957, but only 6.8 per cent after 1957. In 1963, business investment amounted to only 6.7 per cent of gross national product — well below the lowest level of the earlier postwar years. This is no petty change. It represents a decline of 14 per cent in the share of gross national product going into business investment. To put it differently, if business investment in 1963 had been at the 1947–1957 level, instead of at its actual level, $7 billion more would have been spent on new plant and equipment. An additional $7 billion in such expenditures would have made a great difference in the performance of the economy. Among other things, it would have meant a great many more jobs.

It is no accident that business profits, business investment, and unemployment are the three economic indicators that have remained at recession levels throughout the current economic upswing. It takes a lot of business investment to provide one job in the economy of today — indeed, it takes more and more investment for each job. In 1953, American manufacturers had less than $10,000 invested in plant and equipment for each production worker. By 1960, that investment had increased to more than $18,000 per worker. More business investment is needed to provide more jobs for the rapidly growing labor force; the

S.U. Libraries

9

only way to get more investment is to reverse the steady decline in business profits.

The facts are clear. The logic is plain. The need is urgent. We cannot afford to let the facts be obscured, the logic confused, or the need frustrated by a misunderstanding of the positive role of profit in a dynamic economy.

One common misconception is that an increase in cash flow — profits plus depreciation — does as much to stimulate investment as an increase in profit alone. This is simply not the way things work. The decision to invest or not to invest in a company is not based on that company's success in recovering the cost of its past capital outlays. The determining factor is the company's prospects for future profit.

Does this mean that past profit has no influence on present investment? On the contrary, past profit serves as a basis for predicting future earnings. When the general level of profit goes down steadily, as it has in the postwar period, businessmen have the best of reasons for being increasingly conservative in their estimates of the profitability of new investments. The more conservative their estimates, the lower their investments will be, regardless of their cash-flow position.

An even more basic fallacy is the idea that the growth of the economy can be speeded by expanding consumer purchasing power, regardless of the level of profits and investment. The grain of truth behind this argument is the fact that our economy has been operating below its potential in recent years. When this is the case, it may be possible to achieve fuller use of existing capacity to produce simply by stimulating consumer demand.

But fuller use of existing capacity is not economic growth, and it is not enough to satisfy the economic aspirations of the American people. To provide more and more new jobs for our constantly expanding labor force, we need to expand our capacity to produce as well as our capacity to consume. Moreover, in addition to more jobs, we need better, more productive jobs — jobs that will continue to provide the American people with a rising standard of living and a wider variety of new and improved products. All this takes business investment — investment in research and development, investment in new plants, new equipment, new processes, new products. Innovation is both expensive and risky. As often as not, the investment is lost.

Of all the corporations that reported to the Internal Revenue Service during the fiscal year 1962, 40 per cent had operated at a loss — and their losses totaled $6.4 billion. Ours is a profit-and-loss economic system, not a profit system; the chance to make a profit induces people to run the risk of loss. No one with ordinary common sense will risk money on a new idea unless he has good reason to hope for substantial profit — profit commensurate with the risk — if the idea succeeds in the marketplace.

The lower the expected profit for a successful investment, the more new products and processes will be stifled in the boardroom before testing in the marketplace. Conversely, a higher general level of profit on investment will lead to more innovation and economic growth, more and better products for consumers, more and better jobs for employees.

My remarks so far can be summarized in two simple statements. First, profits have been falling steadily. Second, the American people would be better off if profits were higher than they are.

The idea that profit is good is hard for many people to accept. The idea that higher profits are even better is still harder to accept. What the critics of profit see on the surface is that business aims not at helping but at profiting from people. Their instincts tell them that one man's profit is another man's loss, and so they conclude that profit means exploitation. But experience is a better guide than instinct; experience teaches that in a competitive economy businesses profit most from those ventures that best serve the general economic welfare. The target of private business is private profit. The proper target of an economic system is the material well-being of all the people. The great virtue of a free and competitive economy is that it places these two targets in line, so that hitting one means hitting both.

At this point in our national economic history, the target business aims at is becoming steadily smaller and more elusive. Profit is shrinking, and so are the general benefits it brings.

Fortunately, there is reason to hope for some improvement in the profitability of business enterprise. The reduction of federal income taxes, for example, is an important step in the right direction. By cutting taxes across the board, for corporations as well as for individuals in all tax brackets, the tax law of 1964 can increase profit and investment and, simultaneously, stimulate consumer demand. Its first effects on business investment are already being felt. Business plans for new investment in 1964 are up substantially from 1963 and from earlier predictions — it is now expected that business investment in 1964 will be more than $3 billion higher than in 1963 — an increase of 9 per cent.

As encouraging as the present outlook may be, the tax cut is not a panacea. It does not guarantee that profit will rise or that investment will continue to rise. Its benefits could be lost if rising business costs lead either to inflation or to further pressure on profits or to both. Conversely, the benefits of tax reduction can be greatly enhanced if business costs can be reduced.

The responsibility for controlling the rise in business costs is broadly shared. It rests in part with business management; in part with government, state and local as well as federal; in part with employees and their unions; in part with the American people. Management has the primary responsibility for controlling costs by seeking more efficient ways of making and marketing products. But many costs of business lie wholly or partly beyond the control of management. Among them, of course, is the rapidly increasing burden of state and local taxes. To the extent that savings in federal taxes are merely diverted into state and local government treasuries, the benefits of federal tax reduction will be lost.

The federal government has recognized that high tax rates can limit the growth of tax revenues by slowing the growth of the tax base. It has also recognized that the best hope for increasing tax collections in the long run is to limit government spending now and to set taxes at a level that will encourage the growth of the economy. These conclusions are just as relevant to the serious fiscal problems of states and cities as they are to the fiscal problems of the national government. In a broader sense, they are also relevant to the problems of collective bargaining. Recent statements by union leaders suggest that they are planning a determined drive to limit output per worker, to resist management efforts to find more efficient ways of working, and to gain the biggest wage and fringe-benefit increases in many years. Wage costs would also be raised substantially by the Administration's bill to require double time for overtime work in selected industries. The benefits of federal tax reduction can be destroyed just as surely in this manner as by a general increase in state and local taxes. Whether business costs are raised by taxes, by collective bargaining, by new labor legislation, or by other developments, the effects will be the same — lower profits, less investment, slower economic growth, fewer jobs, and lower income for everyone.

On the other hand, whatever serves to reduce costs and restore profit margins will lead to more investment, faster growth, more jobs, and greater income for everyone, including union members.

In the last analysis, much of the responsibility for controlling the rise in business costs belongs to the American people — just as the benefits of lower costs and higher profit belong to them. The taxing power of governments and the bargaining power of unions both are based on law, and law is determined, however imperfectly, by the opinions of the people.

The enactment of the tax law of 1964 is a promising sign that the economic function of profit is gaining broader understanding among the American people and their representatives. It can also promote still broader understanding by demonstrating the benefits higher profit can bring. Those of us in business management face the challenge of proving — not in words, but in deeds — that profit is good and more profit is better. This means, first of all, protecting and enhancing the profits of businesses by a renewed determination to reduce controllable costs. Each of us must run his own shop as efficiently as possible — and then make it still more efficient.

But reducing costs, important as it is, is not the most important part of the challenge we face. The larger responsibility of businessmen is to act in the spirit of the entrepreneur. The entrepreneur dares, he faces the future with boldness and vision, he is ever on the lookout for new markets and new ways to serve old markets. He never passes by a fair chance to make money by risking money. He justifies profit by making it the engine of economic growth and progress. His is the spirit needed to prove that profit is good, not only for business, but for this nation and all its people.

PROFITS IN THE ECONOMY + + +

Editors' Introduction

ANYONE seeking to determine the state of the economy, and to predict future trends, must look closely at the private sector and, notably, at trends in corporate profits. Since there are differing views about the proper measure of profits, great care must be exercised in the use and interpretation of profit figures. The papers in this section, concerned with the development and use of aggregate profit data, enable one to see clearly the limitations of the figures.

In the first paper, Richard Holton discusses the record of profits. After noting some difficulties in measuring profits, he addresses himself to the problem of how best to assess profit performance over time. He cautions that though return on investment is conceptually an attractive measure of profit performance, it has some important limitations. Corporate profit data may include more than pure profit and return for entrepreneurial risks, but may not include executive-incentive compensation and certain other items deducted in the accounting process. Holton further warns that valuational problems distort measures of investment. After citing several studies on returns to net worth, Holton explains that he is not arguing whether profits are too high or too low, but that profits are among the principal engines of economic growth.

Leif Olsen explains the corporate profits series published by the First National City Bank. Using this series he asserts that the absolute level of corporate profits stands at a record high. In his discussion of Dr. Olsen's paper, Dexter Keezer suggests instituting a series on corporate losses. He argues that, since it reflects the experience of the largest and most successful firms, the series on profits does not reveal the experience of the overwhelming number of corporations that suffer losses.

Edmund Mennis discusses the purposes for which information about aggregate profits is needed. Three major measures of profit are distinguished: profits reported to stockholders, profits reported for tax purposes, and profits reported in the national income accounts. After examining several measures of profits, he concludes that for general economic analysis the national income series of the Department of Commerce provides the most useful information. In his second paper, Dr. Mennis reviews the postwar profit record, discusses selection of an appropriate approach to projecting profits, and evaluates the outlook for profit.

RICHARD H. HOLTON

The Record of Profits

THE critical role of profits in a free-enterprise economy is so clear that we need not take time to expand on this basic thought. It would seem unnecessary to preach the profit gospel to this particular congregation — I assume that the brethren here are already saved.

We do hear conflicting stories about the present status of profits in the United States. Corporate profits both before and after taxes are at an all-time high. Yet Henry Ford II has argued that profits are really not at all high compared with selected postwar years, such as 1950. He clearly believes that profit should be higher, by some unspecified margin, than it is now.

The number of alternative measures of profits, or of the performance of profits, is legion. I shall limit myself to *corporate* profits, on the presumption that noncorporate profits must be performing about the same as corporate profits. But even with this simplification, the problems are of course formidable.

There seem to be two principal difficulties. First, How should corporate profits be computed? Edmund Mennis has studied the difference between profits corporations report to their stockholders and profits they report to the Internal Revenue Service. To cite an extreme case, ten petroleum-refining companies reported to the Internal Revenue Service profits equal to just 37.5 per cent of the profits which they reported to their shareholders. For all the companies studied, the net profits after taxes reported to the Internal Revenue Service were just 63 per cent of the profits reported to shareholders. The differences in these figures, I take it, stem largely from differences in depreciation

19

and depletion procedures. It is apparent that profits can be measured in *very* different ways.

Even if the dollars of profits are agreed on, how can one best assess the performance of profits over time? Should one consider profits as a percentage of sales? Profits as a return on net worth? As a return on total investment? Profits as a percentage of the total GNP? As a percentage of the corporate GNP? Here one must decide on some appropriate base, such as net worth, sales, or corporate GNP — and on the appropriate means of measuring that base. This problem is particularly important with respect to net worth.

I shall avoid discussing profits as a percentage of sales. This kind of figure underscores the point that very little of the corporate sales dollar goes to profits, but beyond that it is difficult to make much use of this measure. For example, profits might decrease over time as a percentage of sales but increase as a return on net worth if sales are increasing because of improved plant utilization. Since the stockholder is interested primarily in his investment or his share of the company, presumably the measure of profits as a return on investment is much preferable to that of profits as a percentage of sales.

The rate of return on investment has always been an attractive measure of profit performance. But we might remind ourselves just what is being measured. Corporate profits include some pure profits, i.e., a return to entrepreneurial risk-taking. But they also include some rent and some interest on invested capital. I should include in rent any monopoly return, as when patents are involved. Let me hasten to add that I do not intend the word "monopoly" to have any odious connotations here. After all, the idea of a patent monopoly is accepted policy in this country. Furthermore, there may be some returns which might be included conceptually as corporate profits but which are not reported as profits. The executive-incentive bonus, for example, if not a part of the salary itself, might be considered as profit. Even some of the items on expense accounts might be legitimately included as profits. When profits are being squeezed, firms typically begin to look with much more care at all their costs, including expense accounts. If some expense claims formerly allowed by the auditing staff are now disallowed, these amounts probably should have been included as profits in the first place — they were just paid out to salesmen, executives, or perhaps to customers entertained on expense account funds.

Profits in the Economy

I raise these questions merely for the record — no satisfactory means presently exists for correcting for these many influences on recorded figures of corporate profits. But it is well to remember that the absolute dollars reported as profits are only an approximation to true entrepreneurial profits.

If one talks of corporate profits as a rate of return on investment, then obviously one must measure not only corporate profits for the numerator but investment for the denominator. The problems of valuation here are so obvious and well known that I shall not discuss them.

As to using the return on net worth as the proper measure of profits, what does the record show? Has there been a decrease in profitability in recent years? In 1959 the Machinery and Allied Products Institute (MAPI) compared corporate profits and the rate of return in the 1950's with corporate profits and the rate of return in the 1920's.[1] The corporate profits figures were adjusted for changes in depreciation practices over the years — i.e., depreciation charges were recalculated for recent years assuming straight-line depreciation had been used. The profits also were adjusted so that both depreciation and raw materials were charged to operating expenses on the basis of replacement costs rather than historical costs.

By these MAPI calculations, after-tax profits as a percentage of net worth declined steadily from 1950 through 1954, jumped up again in 1955, and then declined steadily through 1958. The return increased again in 1959 (the figure for 1959 was based on partial data) to a bit under 5 per cent, compared with about 6.5 per cent in 1950. These data are consistent with the argument that the return on investment had declined since 1950 — at least through 1959. (Unfortunately MAPI has not attempted to bring these statistics up to date, so we do not know what the rate of return for the early 1960's would be relative to the 1950's.)

One can argue, of course, that 1950 was scarcely a "normal" year, and so MAPI's adjusted after-tax return of 6.5 per cent for that year was not a good base. The immediate postwar years were unusually prosperous, and competitive pressures were not what they became after the backlog of demand accumulated during the war had been worked off. So it is helpful to reach back to the prewar, pre-depression years for another comparison. The MAPI study compares the average adjusted

[1] Machinery and Allied Products Institute, *Capital Goods Review*, No. 38 (May 1959).

21

rate of return for 1923 through 1929, before and after tax, with the average for 1950 through 1959. The after-tax return is slightly lower in 1950–1959, about 5.5 per cent compared with about 5.75 per cent for 1923–1929. So by this standard, the average for the 1950's, including the 1959 estimated return, is not significantly below the 1920's.

Profits before taxes, with both profits and net worth adjusted by the MAPI method, also show the 1959 return to be well below 1950 — about 10.75 per cent compared with 13 per cent. But the rate of return before tax in the 1950's was well above that for the 1920's — 11 per cent compared with about 6.5 per cent.

MAPI concludes: "after appropriate adjustments, recent pre-tax profits have represented a much higher margin on adjusted net worth, and after-tax profits about the same margin" as in the 1920's.[2]

George Stigler [3] has examined rates returned on net worth for *manufacturing* corporations, without any of the MAPI adjustments. These show after-tax profits as a rate of return again declining since the early 1950's, but by the late 1950's they were fluctuating roughly in the range of 5 to 7 per cent, as they were in 1926–1929.

So much for the record of profits measured as a percentage rate of return on investment. Let us now turn to corporate profits as a share of the gross national product. In 1963 profits before taxes, including inventory evaluation adjustment, were 8.7 per cent of the GNP, down from 10.1 per cent in 1947, 12.5 per cent in 1950, and 9.8 per cent in 1959. Profits after taxes show the same general pattern.

Some of this decline in share might be attributed to a decline in the corporate share of the GNP. But Robert E. Graham and Jacqueline Bauman have examined corporate profits before taxes, including inventory evaluation adjustment as a percentage of the corporate GNP since 1947. Their study, published in the *Survey of Current Business*, November 1962, shows quite clearly that this share has declined markedly, from 21.3 per cent in the last half of 1948 to 15.7 per cent in the first half of 1962. In 1963 the share slipped a bit further, to 14.9 per cent.

It is interesting to see what shares of the corporate GNP increased at the expense of corporate profits. Compensations of employees (wages and salaries plus supplements) stood at 64 per cent of the corporate

[2] *Ibid.*, p. 4.
[3] *Capital and Rates of Return in Manufacturing Industries* (National Bureau of Economic Research; Princeton, N.J.: Princeton University Press, 1963), p. 203.

GNP in both years. So the profits share of the corporate GNP has not declined because of a rising share going to labor. Indirect taxes (largely state and local taxes) increased from 8.9 per cent of the corporate GNP in 1948 to 10.5 per cent in 1962 and to 10.8 per cent in 1963. The really big increase, however, was in the capital consumption allowances; these are, of course, depreciation charges. Depreciation increased from 5.5 per cent of the corporate GNP in the last half of 1948 to 9.5 per cent in the first half of 1962. In 1963, depreciation moved up to a full 10 per cent of the corporate GNP. So the depreciation share of the corporate GNP rose by 4 percentage points, direct taxes rose by 1.6 percentage points, and the profits share fell by just about the sum of these two figures.

The rise in depreciation charges has not received adequate attention in discussions of the postwar "profit squeeze." Yet this rise is indeed dramatic. While the corporate GNP rose from $143.4 billion in the second half of 1948 to $305.7 billion in the first half of 1962, an increase of about 112 per cent, capital consumption allowances increased from $8.0 billion to $28.9 billion, an increase of 261 per cent. Depreciation charges in the early postwar years were low because the capital plant of the country was unusually old, given the wartime deferment of much plant modernization, and of course the historical cost was far below replacement cost, so corporate profits were grossly overstated. "Capital stocks grew more rapidly than output during the post-war period, and comparatively short-lived equipment, which carries a high annual depreciation quota, increased relative to structures, which have longer service lives and consequently lower annual depreciation." [4]

In an article in the October 1963 *Survey of Current Business*, Murray Brown of the Office of Business Economics in the Department of Commerce has recomputed corporate profits before and after taxes, using alternative sets of assumptions with respect to depreciation methods. The national income version of corporate profits shows an increase of 61 per cent in corporate profits before taxes — from $30.0 billion in 1948 to $48.4 billion in 1963. (Brown's published data extend only through 1962, but the 1963 values have been calculated.) If straight-line depreciation on a basis of current cost had been used throughout the time period covered, corporate profits would have increased by 83

---

[4] Murray Brown, "Depreciation in Corporate Profits," *Survey of Current Business*, XLIII, No. 10 (October 1963), 7, 8.

per cent. Using the after-tax profits, the national income version shows an increase of 39 per cent between 1948 and 1963, while standardized methods of straight-line depreciation on a basis of current costs would have shown corporate profits increasing by 74 per cent.

What of corporate profits as a percentage of income originating in the corporate sector? Even using the profits derived from straight-line depreciation on a basis of current cost, one finds that corporate profits as a percentage of income originating in the corporate sector declined from 22.7 per cent in 1948 to 18.8 per cent in 1963.

Most of us are interested in profits after taxes. Using straight-line depreciation on a basis of current cost, corporate profits after taxes in 1963 accounted for about 9.5 per cent of income originating in the corporate sector. This was a larger percentage than in any year since 1950, excepting 1950 itself and 1955, when the percentages were 10.3 per cent and 10.1 per cent respectively.

In other words, in only two of the previous fourteen years did corporate profits do better, by this particular measure, than in 1963. Yet if we look at the national income version of this measure, we see that in seven of these fourteen years the profit performance matched, or bettered, the 1963 performance. Surely for purposes of analyzing the record of profits, one is well advised to adjust for changing depreciation practices. And when that is done, the profits performance in 1963 was a creditable one.

Perhaps the importance of adjusting for changes in depreciation practices can best be illustrated by two contrasting figures. Mr. Ford has indicated that when the record-breaking profits of 1963 are converted to 1950 dollars, they shrink from $27 billion to $20.5 billion — 10 per cent below the actual profits of American corporations in 1950. Yet if depreciation practices had been standardized over the time period covered, using the straight-line basis of current cost, corporate profits after taxes would have increased, in terms of price-corrected dollars, by about 37 per cent from 1950 to 1963.

This contrast underscores the significance of the adjustment of the profit record for changes in depreciation practices and for changes in the price level of the plant and equipment being replaced. In the early 1950's the business community was complaining, and quite properly so, that corporate profits were seriously overstated because depreciation was understated. The data which I have been using have been corrected for that understatement of depreciation. Adoption of the various accelerated depreciation formulas has increased depreciation charges in recent years. The data I have used have also been adjusted for the new depreciation formulas. Surely it must be recognized that when more lenient depreciation practices have been permitted and widely adopted in business, the effect of the faster write-offs is, at least for a time, to raise depreciation charges and hence to reduce profits.

In closing, I beg the reader not to misinterpret the thrust of my paper. I am not trying to argue that profits are now too high; nor am I trying to argue that profits are now too low. On this point my paper is neutral. We must certainly recognize that profits are one of the principal engines of economic growth, and we must see to it that the prospect for profit is bright enough in this country to assure continued economic expansion. But in discussing the record of profits, let us not be misled by overstated or understated profit data.

+ + +   LEIF H. OLSEN

The Economic Performance of Corporations

I SHOULD like to begin by saying a few things about the corporate profits series which the First National City Bank compiles and publishes. Second, I shall discuss some concepts of corporate profits and depreciation charges, and third, I shall comment on some relations among corporate profits, cash flow, and factors influencing expenditures for plant and equipment.

I represent an institution that has long had a special interest in providing a better understanding of corporate profits. Indeed, it has been more than three decades since the first issue of the bank's detailed annual review of corporate profits, covering at the start 709 corporations and now covering nearly 4,000. In addition to this review, which appears in the *Monthly Economic Letter* each April, the bank also publishes quarterly tabulations for a smaller group of corporations, now totaling approximately 1,000, in the March, May, August, and November issues of the *Letter*. The figures come directly from corporate reports to stockholders.

From the outset, one of the primary objectives of the corporate profits series was to make information on corporate profits available as soon as possible after results for each year are reported. This gives an advantage in timeliness over some of the governmental estimates of profits that cover more companies, provide various adjustments of the data, and, therefore, take longer to compile.

In April 1964 were published the 1963 results for 3,934 companies, showing total profits of $26.4 billion, up 9 per cent from 1962. This figure accounts for approximately 97 per cent of total corporate profits as estimated on a different basis for national income accounts. However, I should stress, as does the *Monthly Economic Letter*, that the companies in the survey include the largest and most successful in the country, and consequently the figures do not fully reflect the overwhelming number of corporations that lost money even in a good business year like 1963.

The average rate of return on net worth for all corporations in the survey was 9.5 per cent in 1963, the highest since 1959. Perhaps of greater interest is the fact that the return on net worth showed an increase for the second year in a row, the first time in fifteen years that the bank's figures for return on net worth have grown two years in a row. Of course, like all averages, that return on net worth hides a fairly wide range, which in this case runs from a low of 3 per cent for the amusement industry to a high of 20 per cent for automobile manufacturers.

Profit margins on sales similarly showed the same unusual increase two years in a row, though it is a modest gain of .4 per cent—from 5.5 per cent in 1961 to 5.9 per cent in 1963—for nonfinancial corporations in the survey.

The bank makes available upon request the annual returns on net worth for the years since 1925, and net profit margins for the years since 1933. These figures are broken down for sixty-five to seventy classifications of industries for the years since 1947, and for a smaller number of classifications for the years from the beginning of the series in 1928 to 1947.

The bank also publishes quarterly the percentage of total reporting companies which show an increase in after-tax profits, a series used by the National Bureau of Economic Research as one of its leading indicators. This proportion dipped slightly to 55 per cent in the fourth quarter from 56 per cent in the third and 59 per cent in the second. These moderate changes are not particularly significant. However, the figures themselves certainly point up that even in this cream-of-the-crop survey, profit gains for any one period are by no means evenly distributed. I believe it vital to keep this in mind when by necessity one examines and analyzes total figures.

Another product of the corporate profits analysis is the quarterly compilation of a seasonally adjusted index of corporate profits based on a sample that has grown from 400 to 900 leading manufacturing corporations and adjusted to annual data for 1,700 corporations in the early years and for 2,300 more recently. This seasonally adjusted index provides a more accurate picture of changes in the level of corporate profits over a period of time than that obtained from the total survey, which, of course, is not seasonally adjusted and in which the number of corporations changes somewhat from one survey to the next.

The bank does not now publish this quarterly index but is considering doing so after some further refinement and thereby making it generally available. In addition, the bank hopes to broaden the processing of the raw material published by a large and highly significant number of corporations, in order to extract additional information of help and interest not only to itself but to others devoted to analyzing and improving the understanding of corporate profits in our economy.

I suggest that the interest in profits is particularly timely because the absolute level of corporate profits stands at a record high, having grown by about 10 per cent in 1962 and in 1963 with the promise of a third gain of about this magnitude in 1964. Naturally, corporate profits at this level attract much wider attention than do corporate profits in those years when they show little change. As might well be expected, a great many of the people who concentrate on corporate profits in such times as these do not understand the true nature of corporate profits or fail to be circumspect in their analysis of the rise of these earnings because of preconceived ideas about appropriate or inappropriate distribution of profits before and after taxes. So it follows that disagreement and misunderstanding of the level and purpose of corporate profits become particularly visible at times when those profits are high and growing higher.

Successful individuals in our society can, if they wish, elect to enjoy quiet prosperity — the kind that doesn't attract too much attention in the community. But the successful publicly owned corporations, especially those listed on the national securities exchanges, have no such chance to obscure their financial performances, nor should they. But the point is that the successful corporation often draws to it the antagonism of those — and the number is by no means small — who view rising corporate profits with suspicion and who at some point are prone to say profits are excessive. Others believe reported profits are not high enough, suspecting that substantial profits are being concealed, and still others insist that growing profits are being unwisely employed or unfairly distributed.

Thus, labor believes it is not getting a fair share of before-tax income, some stockholders believe a larger portion of after-tax profits should be paid out in dividends, and still others insist that more should be retained in the business for capital investment. Tax collectors at all levels of government, of course, have their claims to make. I am sure this is only a partial list of those who insist on the right to say how corporate income should be distributed. Finally, however, corporate managers and directors concerned with the future well-being of the corporation, its growth and competitive strength, must decide how to allocate income left after payment of fixed charges and expenses. Unfortunately these men cannot satisfy everyone, nor should they be expected to.

In this context, the recent reduction in corporate- and personal-income-tax rates represents an effort to stimulate greater economic growth by shifting a substantial amount of spending power from the government to the private sector, a somewhat unusual experience. The consideration that led to the investment tax credit, new depreciation guidelines, and reduction of corporate tax rates reflected a changing attitude of the government toward corporate capital investment and its contribution to economic performance. The extent to which this change in attitude has penetrated other areas of our society remains to be tested, by such means as labor negotiations in some of our major industries.

This brings me to my second point. In recent years the understanding of corporate profits has been influenced in no small way by widespread attention to depreciation charges and after-tax profits, or what is generally called gross cash flow. Charges to cover the depreciation of plant and equipment have grown substantially since the end of World War II: depreciation charges have risen from $5 billion or 28 per cent of gross cash flow in 1947 to $29 billion or 57 per cent of cash flow in 1963 (from estimates based on Federal Reserve flow-of-funds figures for all nonfinancial corporations). Such a rise has brought this question: Do depreciation charges cause an understatement of "true" profits? A growing body of opinion holds that they do.

Whereas many have described the development of this opinion among some security analysts, I should like to put it in slightly different words: In the early postwar years when a relatively bearish or cautious sentiment characterized the stock market, it was popular to believe that corporate profits were overstated. There was merit to this idea because, although prices were rising, depreciation charges based on original cost of plant and equipment were inadequate to cover postwar replacement cost. Today, with price-earnings ratios historically high and a generally bullish sentiment dominating the market, the picture has changed. Profits are now claimed to be understated because depreciation charges are said to be excessive.

However, I should agree with Perry Mason, late director of Accounting Research at the American Institute of Certified Public Accountants, that "Unless it can be shown that depreciation rates being employed by industry are inaccurate and unreasonably high, or that improper accounting methods are being used, there is no defensible basis for saying that 'much of the profit margin squeeze is artificial because one of the most rapidly increasing cost items is depreciation . . .' and that 'corporate profits today are being understated as never before.'"[1] In reading such statements from time to time, I have yet to find a valid analysis discrediting depreciation charges.

The misconception of the source and purpose of cash flow arose from a fundamental misunderstanding of the economic arguments involved. If an investment is to be profitable, the excess of sales revenues over current expenses must be large enough to permit the recovery of the invested capital and provide an adequate profit. It is quite true that the separation of recovery of capital from profit is somewhat arbitrary, but this does not lead to the conclusion that the profit squeeze has been illusory. There is good reason to believe that depreciation charges are now a reasonably good measure of the amount of capital that must be recovered each year. And there is no reason to believe that more than a relatively minor portion of the increase in depreciation charges results from tax law and regulation changes which have allowed the transfer of the accounting charge to the depreciation line instead of the profits line.

An article appearing in the October 1963 issue of the *Survey of Current Business* showed that corporate profits plus depreciation in the aggregate have been steadily declining since the early 1950's as a percentage of corporate gross product. Moreover, no matter what method

[1] *Cash Flow Analysis and the Funds Statement* (New York: American Institute of Certified Public Accountants, 1962), p. 37.

of depreciation is used, the most or the least rapid, a squeeze on the resulting net profit figure is still evident.

During the years since World War II ended, nonfinancial corporations in the United States have spent $404 billion for plant and equipment (this is based on Federal Reserve flow-of-funds figures). It is not surprising, then, to see a sharp rise in depreciation charges against income, reflecting reductions in the value of these fixed assets purchased during the period of sharply rising prices.

The implication that the cash from depreciation charges can be diverted painlessly into higher wages or dividends is a myth. The money cannot be given to labor without making investment less attractive to the stockholder. It cannot be given to the stockholder without reducing the capital of the firm and causing it to shrink. While it may conceivably be true that the stockholder can reinvest this money more profitably than can the firm, this is hardly the argument security analysts had in mind when they developed the cash-flow approach. They are, after all, great believers in the future growth of corporate earnings per share, and such growth cannot usually be maintained without increases in investment.

It is not uncommon to see figures for net cash flow (that is, depreciation plus cash retained from earnings) compared with expenditures for plant and equipment. Indeed these figures are brought together with those for plant and equipment so often as to suggest that rising internally generated funds would by themselves quickly lead to rising expenditures for plant and equipment and that, if this is not the case, corporate managements are simply behaving somewhat like the king in his countinghouse, counting out his money. Cash flow was greater than plant and equipment expenditures for the three years 1961–1963, which is significant (I shall say more about it later) but not extraordinary. The broad implication of this comparison, namely, that corporations are waxing fat, can be quite misleading.

The bank estimates that cash flow of nonfinancial corporations exceeded plant and equipment expenditures not only in 1961–1963, but also in 1959, in 1955, and notably in the four years ending with 1951. And of course in no year did depreciation charges exceed plant and equipment expenditures.

Such comparisons alone actually tell little about corporate behavior. Cash flow plays only the passive role of providing a readily tapped source of funds. Some, it is true, must be used to replace capital. But some of the depreciation charges of a growing firm are being set aside for future replacements and must be invested in the interim; if profitable opportunities exist, these investments can be and usually are made within the firm. Retained earnings exist solely to make some form of investment for the stockholder — be it in working capital, fixed investment, or debt retirement. To evaluate corporate performance, one must therefore consider how this cash flow is distributed among alternative uses. In a favorable year, firms will use a large proportion of the funds on fixed investments and go to the capital market for additional funds. In less favorable years, however, though firms will still find it desirable to reinvest this money, they will do so by directly or indirectly supplying funds to the capital market. In recent years, for example, corporations have turned to such alternate avenues as financing receivables and extending trade credit, which help volume of sales and yield a return at the same time.

This brings me to my third point. There is no doubt that corporations have been spending less for plant and equipment in recent years than they have been capable of on the basis of internally generated funds. Some comparisons of the years before and after 1957 are worthy of note. From 1947 to 1957 after-tax corporate profits of nonfinancial corporations increased by an average annual rate of 1 per cent, cash flow by 6.2 per cent, and plant and equipment expenditures by 8.2 per cent. From 1957 to 1963 the average annual rise in corporate profits was 2.9 per cent, in cash flow 7.4 per cent, and in plant and equipment expenditures .1 per cent. Plant and equipment spending grew much less than corporate profits and cash flow. Of course the picture for 1964 appears to be changing, but I shall discuss that later.

Why have corporations slowed their investment in plant and equipment in recent years? There are those who suggest that the great rise in cash flow should have effected a much sharper gain in capital investment. However, the ability to finance capital investment is not synonymous with the willingness to do so.

A good many studies have been undertaken to determine the relative importance of influences on plant and equipment expenditures. Understandably, there have been differences of opinion. However, I believe it fair to say that the largest body of opinion holds that expectation of profit, or, to put it another way, expectation of increasing the profitability of the companies, is the most important factor leading to capital investment. The debate centers on what developments influence profit expectations the most. It has been said that in their calculations to arrive at such expectations businessmen must attempt to anticipate changes in demand, technology, and a variety of other strategic variables such as wage rates, cost of borrowed money, taxes, and government regulatory policies.

Although much work remains to be done, economists — armed with a battery of mathematical and statistical tools — have attempted to measure the relative importance of the influences on business investment in plant and equipment. These studies seem to imply two alternative conclusions. One view, represented most notably by Robert Eisner, is that evidence from both the prewar and the postwar periods strongly indicates that capital spending is largely determined by changes in demand or sales and that recent profits by themselves provide little additional explanation of fluctuations in investment or differences from one industry to another in rates of expansion. This approach has frequently emphasized sustained movements of demand rather than current changes alone. Other economists have given more weight to profits. One of the most recent studies, "Capital and Rates of Return in Manufacturing Industries," directed by George Stigler and published by the National Bureau of Economic Research, agrees that changes in demand have considerably influenced business decisions to invest. However, Stigler also finds that over a reasonably long period of time, with adjustment for price changes, differences among industries in rates of growth of total assets are more readily accounted for by interindustry differences in profitability or rates of return than by changes in demand. Especially interesting and suggestive is Stigler's finding that efficiency tends to increase more rapidly in industries with high rates of return than in those with relatively low rates.

The somewhat tentative nature of much of the research, limited as it is by the relatively short time span for which there are good data, should discourage the economist from attempting to draw firm conclusions. Even many of the studies emphasizing current profits as a determinant of investment tend to leave open the question of whether it is profits per se or the availability of cash that is really important. But regardless of the uncertainty about the relative importance of particular factors, virtually all the evidence is fully consistent with one over-

riding principle: the fundamental stimulus to investment is its anticipated profitability.

It is not my purpose in citing these findings by economists to question their validity or to favor any one above the others. I am sure that
in the actual decision-making in the boardroom all these factors play a
part. Although some writers emphasize anticipated demand and others
current or recent return or profitability as forces shaping decisions to
invest in fixed assets, I would call attention to the close correlation between the rate of return on net assets and the degree of utilization of
capacity for manufacturing companies. During the 1950's these two followed an almost identical pattern. However, from 1960 through the
current expansion cycle it appears that increases in output relative to
capacity have not generated the same proportionate rise in return on
net worth that seemed evident in earlier years. The very gentle increase
in rate of return and in utilization of capacity in this unusually long
expansion cycle has also been accompanied by an only moderate rise in
plant and equipment expenditures, despite the sharp increase in cash
flow.

In the present cycle with its moderate rise in demand relative to
capacity and slow rise in return on net worth, it is not surprising to find
that plant and equipment expenditures have been growing at a slower
rate than in previous postwar expansions. However, if plans are fulfilled in 1964, this fourth year of the current expansion, the rate of increase in capital spending will top that of any year since 1956. No small
credit can be given to the tax cut in improving expectations for future
demand and profits.

The rise beginning in 1961 in the return on net worth has been moderate, to be sure, but it is significant that a gain in 1964 will set a record
of three increases in a row for manufacturing corporations (according
to First National City Bank figures). This is the first time for an increase
of this duration since the years 1945–1948. The current improvement,
moreover, does not reflect excessive demand or inflationary pressures
but economic circumstances quite different from those of the early postwar years. The 1960's thus far are clear of the economic influences of
the upheaval of depression and war.

There is perhaps an atmosphere of expectancy among economists
that this decade will provide better data and experience to test and to
prove or disprove some of the economic ideas that were necessarily

based on events stemming from the thirty years which encompassed depression, war, and postwar events. New insights and, of course, the computer should enable economists in this period to make great strides in applying economic analysis to our problems and aspirations.

Comments   DEXTER M. KEEZER

MY COMMENTS are addressed to the theme of understanding profits. I don't mind in the least that Mr. Olsen devoted the first third of his paper to a commercial for the series on profits of the First National City Bank. He's entitled to do so. The First National City series is a great series, and it's a tremendous help to all of us. But the United States Department of the Treasury reports that during all of the prosperous 1950's about 40 per cent of the active corporations in the United States lost money. This fact suggests that as a companion piece for the series on profits the First National City Bank should have an annual series on losses. This would put the series on profits — and it is used extensively in educational institutions — in proper perspective.

I want to make one other point. I agree thoroughly with Mr. Olsen's distinguishing of cash flow and profits and the conceptions of them. This means that I disagree completely with the *American Federationist*, the official magazine of the AFL-CIO, which recently argued, "The cash flow, which is reported profits plus depreciation allowances, is the accurate measure of a company's returns, since it's the amount of money left over after the payment of all costs and taxes."[1] If that becomes the accepted conception of profits or business returns, it will be a most effective way of getting rid of the business system. Depreciation is a cost; it's not what is left over after all payments of costs and taxes, and acting as if it were leads to tremendous trouble.

I believe Mr. Olsen is right when he asserts that there is good reason to believe that depreciation charges are now a reasonably good measure of the amount of capital that must be recovered each year — that is, if the company doesn't choose to liquidate. But to make this understood, I think we'd be vastly better off if we limited depreciation allowances to offsetting the actual wear and tear and obsolescence, instead of per-

[1] *American Federationist*, LXIX (June 1962).

mitting the taxing authorities to push allowances up or down to stimulate or discourage business investments in capital equipment. This is an idea; I assume that there are experts who can handle the technical details of applying such a policy.

This reminds me of the centipede that suffered from corns. He learned that the bee was a very wise creature. So he went to him and said, "I need some advice. What can I do about relieving my corns?" The bee replied, "If I were you, I'd get myself turned into a spider. You'd have far fewer legs and far fewer corns." "That's an admirable idea," said the centipede. "How can I do it?" The bee responded, "I advise only on policy." Well, that's my situation: I've advised a policy: I hope you experts follow it.

+ + +   EDMUND A. MENNIS

Measuring Aggregate Corporate Profits

IN A profit-oriented economy such as that of the United States, the trends of and prospects for corporate profits are vital in determining how well the economic system is working. Business prospects and the profit outlook are strongly intertwined. Nevertheless, it is remarkable, on reviewing the literature, to see how little work has been done and how widespread is the misunderstanding of the problems and methods of profit measurement. Therefore, it is useful here both to consider the purposes for which information about aggregate profits is needed and to differentiate among the various profit measures available to meet these needs.

PURPOSE OF CORPORATE PROFITS INFORMATION

Chief users of information about profits are the economist, the businessman, and the financial analyst. The economist may want such information for a number of reasons: to appraise the general health of the economy; to evaluate the incentive for capital investment; to measure dividend disbursements and the savings from retained earnings; to compute the profits on which taxes will be paid, thus providing federal revenue; to appraise the cyclical status of profits, which have been designated by the National Bureau of Economic Research as a leading indicator of business-cycle turning points. The businessman watches profits trends in order to estimate the general outlook for business, to evaluate the performance of his own industry and those of his customers and suppliers, and also to measure the performance of his own company against that of its competitors. The needs of the financial analyst are somewhat the same as both the economist's and the businessman's, although he concentrates more on trends in profits and their evaluation in the securities markets. Consequently, he seeks some profit series that can be related to security prices. The financial analyst may also compare the profit performance of a particular company with that of an industry or with some other aggregate profit measure.

Unfortunately, no one available profit measure meets all these diverse needs. The appropriate series can be selected after considering the basic types of profit data and the various sources of the time series available.

BASIC DATA AVAILABLE

Three basic types of profit measures may be distinguished: profits reported to shareholders, profits reported for tax purposes, and profits reported in the national income accounts. These three types of profits differ significantly, but only the highlights of these differences can be discussed here.[1]

Shareholder Reports. For the individual company, profits reported to shareholders are the most familiar and the most widely quoted. This measure of profits reflects managerial evaluation of the operations of the company, the results of which ordinarily are checked by an annual independent audit. Some problems arise in totaling profits figures from reports of individual companies because accounting procedures may vary from company to company or even within the same company over a period of time. This difficulty is illustrated by the example of two companies in the same kind of business, each with $10 million in sales, and each using generally accepted accounting methods. The net profit reported for the first company was $430,000 and for the second $1,076,000, the difference arising solely from variations in accounting treatment and not from any factors affecting the operation of the business.[2]

Nevertheless, admitting reporting differences among companies, profits from shareholder reports have one thing in common: from the point

[1] For a more complete discussion, see Edmund A. Mennis, "Different Measures of Corporate Profits," *Financial Analysts Journal*, XVIII, No. 5 (September–October 1962), 69–78.

[2] T. A. Wise, "The Auditors Have Arrived," *Fortune*, LXII, No. 6 (December 1960), 145. A more detailed description of the impact of varying accounting treatment upon reported profits under "generally accepted accounting principles" is contained in an article by David Norr, "Accounting and Analysis," *Financial Analysts Journal*, XX (May–June 1964), 38–45.

of view of businessman, shareholder, or financial analyst, the audited opinions of management are the final determinants of the earnings of a company and, therefore, a major determinant of dividend policy. Moreover, although not subject to statistical proof, my experience as a financial analyst suggests that these earnings and dividends, as reported, are important in determining stock prices and, accordingly, the state of business and consumer confidence.

Tax Returns. In addition to reporting to shareholders, management is required to submit to the Internal Revenue Service an annual report of its operations. These reports have far greater uniformity than have reports to shareholders because they must conform to the Internal Revenue Code. However, complete uniformity is not found here either because of the varying accounting treatment permitted under the Code for items that may be either capitalized or expensed — such as inventories, depreciation, and outlays. Tax reports of individual companies are, of course, not made public, because the Internal Revenue Service is required by law to keep the returns of individual companies confidential; however, it annually publishes a detailed compilation of corporate-tax returns by industry and in the aggregate in its *Statistics of Income.* The time lag in the publishing of these figures is one of their greatest drawbacks; they are generally available about two years after the tax year. Consequently, income tax data are of no help for current analysis, although they have been quite valuable for longer, historical studies.

There has been little analysis of the difference between profits reported to shareholders and profits reported for tax purposes. However, a special study in 1961 [3] suggested that profits reported to shareholders are not statistically comparable with profits reported for tax purposes. Methods of treatment of consolidation and depreciation are the main reasons for these differences. Many large corporations with foreign subsidiaries now report to shareholders on a fully consolidated, worldwide

[3] Mennis, "Different Measures of Corporate Profits," pp. 70–72. In an earlier study by Dan T. Smith and J. Keith Butters, *Taxable and Business Income* (New York: National Bureau of Economic Research, 1949), a detailed analysis was made of the differences between book profit and statutory net income reported on tax returns for the prewar years 1929–1936. The authors concluded that a comparison of book profit and audited statutory net income indicated that the two figures tended to be about equal in most industries for the period studied. Changes in tax laws and corporate accounting practices since World War II seem to indicate a modification of this conclusion.

basis, although their income tax reports reflect only the operations of the domestic parent company plus foreign dividends remitted, if any. The changes in depreciation permitted under the revenue acts of 1954, 1962, and 1964 have been particularly important. Many industrial companies have increased the depreciation taken on their tax books but have not increased their depreciation reported to stockholders to the same extent.[4] Consequently, although broad aggregates of profits reported to shareholders and to tax collectors may tend to move together, significant variations may occur, especially if the analysis is extended to more detailed industry comparisons.

National Income Profits. The third basic profit series is that reported in the national income accounts issued by the Office of Business Economics, Department of Commerce. A casual reader of this figure in the newspaper might think that it represented the addition of all of the profit figures for individual companies that are reported and published quarterly. Such is not the case. Rather, the corporate profit figure of the Department of Commerce is an attempt to measure the earnings of corporations that accrue to the residents of the nation as part of the aggregate earnings of labor and property arising from current production in the nation.

The Department of Commerce bases its estimates, first of all, on profits reported for the income tax. Second, certain adjustments are made to this estimate of profits in order to conform to definitions of national income. The Department of Commerce seeks to measure corporate earnings accruing to residents of the United States without deduction of depletion charges and exclusive of capital gains and losses. Intercorporate dividends also are eliminated, and net receipts of dividends and branch profits from abroad to all residents of the United States are added. In addition, an estimate of profits subsequently to

[4] This fact can be demonstrated by comparing the change from 1961 to 1962 in depreciation by industry as reported by the Department of Commerce (*Survey of Current Business*, XLIII (July 1963), p. 4, Table I) with the change in depreciation for the same years for manufacturing corporations as reported by the Federal Trade Commission–Securities and Exchange Commission in its *Quarterly Financial Report for Manufacturing Corporations*. The report of the Department of Commerce reflected an estimate of the depreciation to be used in tax reports, and the FTC-SEC report reflected depreciation used in shareholder reports. The percentage increase in depreciation in tax reports in almost all industries was more than double the increase shown in reports to shareholders. Even allowing for the conceptual differences between the two series, the differences in depreciation appear significant.

40

be disclosed by audit is added. All of these adjustments amount to more than 30 per cent of the taxable profit figure.

SOURCES OF INFORMATION

For information about these three basic types of data, the analyst can choose among a number of statistical series of aggregate profits. Five of the commonly used detailed aggregates of profits are summarized in the comparison on p. 42. The sources of these reports are as follows:

1. Internal Revenue Service: This report is the annual compilation of income tax returns of all corporations in the United States prepared by the Internal Revenue Service of the United States Department of the Treasury and published in *Statistics of Income, Corporate Income Tax Returns.*

2. Department of Commerce: This report consists of annual compilations by industry of profits of all corporations, prepared for the national income accounts and published by the Office of Business Economics of the United States Department of Commerce. The data are published each year in the July issue of the *Survey of Current Business.* Detailed historical data are also found in *U.S. Income and Output,* the 1958 supplement to the *Survey of Current Business.* In addition, quarterly estimates are published of total profits before and after taxes and inventory valuation adjustment as well as of profits (before taxes) and inventory valuation adjustment for major sections of (1) durable and nondurable manufacturing; (2) transportation, communications, and public utilities; (3) all other industries. All of these series are reported at seasonally adjusted annual rates with a two- to four-month time lag in the *Survey of Current Business* and in the *Economic Indicators.*

3. FTC-SEC: This report is the *Quarterly Financial Report for Manufacturing Corporations* prepared by the Federal Trade Commission–Securities and Exchange Commission.

4. First National City Bank: This report is compiled quarterly by the bank from reports to shareholders and published in the March, May, August, and November issues of the *Monthly Economic Letter* of the First National City Bank, New York. The April issue presents a more detailed tabulation and analysis of annual data.

5. Federal Reserve: This quarterly report covers a selected group of

Comparison of Detailed Reports of Corporate Profits

Data Included	Income Tax Returns		Shareholder Reports		Federal Reserve
	Internal Revenue Service	Department of Commerce	FTC-SEC	First National City Bank	
Coverage	All companies	All companies	All manufacturing companies	Quarterly, about 900; annually, about 3,800 leading companies	177 large manufacturing companies; Class I railroads; utilities; Bell Telephone System
Frequency	Annually	Annually[a]	Quarterly	Quarterly	Quarterly
Time lag	2 years	2 years[a]	3–4 months	1–2 months	3 months
Industry classification	Mostly 2-digit basis[b]	2-digit basis[b]	2- to 4-digit basis[b]	Mostly 3-digit basis[b]	6 major manufacturing groups; rails, utilities, Bell Telephone System
Consistent sample over time	No	No	No	No	Yes
Accounting detail	Income account and balance sheet	Sales, pretax, taxes, net, dividends, depreciation	Income account and balance sheet	Net income, net assets	Sales, pretax, net, dividends
Accounting treatment of					
Capital gains and losses	Included	Excluded	Excluded	Included	Excluded
Special reserves	Excluded	Excluded	Excluded	Included	Excluded
Foreign subsidiary earnings	Dividends only	Excluded[c]	Included as reported	Included as reported	Included as reported
Intercorporate dividends	Included	Excluded	Included	Included	Excluded if identified

[a] Estimates of seasonally adjusted annual rates of total corporate profits and three of the major components are also available quarterly with a two- to four-month time lag.

[b] In *Standard Industrial Classification Manual.*

[c] Although not shown by industry, a "rest of the world" adjustment indicates the net effect of corporate profits and dividends received from abroad by both corporations and individuals in the United States less corporate profits and dividends paid abroad.

manufacturing companies as well as Class I railroads, Class A and B electric utilities, and the Bell Telephone System. Data are published monthly in the *Federal Reserve Bulletin*.

DETAIL AND COMPARABILITY OF PROFIT SERIES

As indicated in the comparison on p. 42, two of the reports (those of the Internal Revenue Service and the Department of Commerce) draw data from income tax returns, the other three from company reports to shareholders.

Industry Detail. The industrial detail in many of the reports is based on the industry classifications in the *Standard Industrial Classification Manual*, published by the United States Bureau of the Budget. The structure of industrial classification in this manual is in progressively more detailed categories, using two-, three-, and four-digit numbers as bases. Ordinarily, a two-digit classification is so broad as to have limited use for financial comparisons of industries. Moreover, definitions of industry classifications have changed several times in the postwar period, so that comparisons over time sometimes cannot be made. Because the industry definitions occasionally differ from those generally used in the financial field, an analyst is well advised to check the definition in the manual before using any series for comparison.

Consistency of Sample. When interpreting changes in the results over time, an analyst must consider whether the same group of companies constitutes the sample or whether the shifting composition of the sample itself changes the results. The series of the Department of Commerce and that in *Statistics of Income* are so broad that, for all practical purposes, they reflect the activities of all corporations — though not, of course, the same corporations from year to year. The FTC–SEC sample changes each quarter; therefore, although the sample represents the entire manufacturing sector, quarterly totals are not strictly addable to obtain annual results. In addition, mergers, especially of large companies in different industrial classifications, may affect the comparability of data from quarter to quarter for particular industries if a major company has been moved from one classification to another.

The series of the First National City Bank covers companies that publish regular financial reports; the companies included are only those whose reports are in hand when the *Monthly Economic Letter* goes to press. Consequently, the series is not consistent from quarter to quarter, although the bank has prepared a seasonally adjusted link-relative index of net income on a quarterly basis, available upon request. The Federal Reserve series is the only one that contains the same companies over the entire period for which it is available.

Accounting Detail. Accounting detail given also varies; only the FTC–SEC report and the *Statistics of Income* provide balance-sheet data. The accounting adjustments vary considerably; only the First National City Bank uses reports to shareholders without adjustments or arbitrary modifications. Treatment of foreign earnings is especially limited in the series of *Statistics of Income* and the Department of Commerce, with only remitted dividends included in *Statistics of Income* and with foreign dividends entirely excluded from the industrial data in the series of the Department of Commerce. The latter series lumps foreign dividends and corporate profits from abroad together in a "Rest of the World" sector, and nets them out against domestic corporate dividends paid to foreign stockholders and profits of domestic branches of foreign corporations.

PROFITS DATA FOR FINANCIAL ANALYSIS

Further sources of comparative data of interest primarily to the financial analyst should be mentioned.

Standard & Poor's. Standard & Poor's Corporation has published annual earnings per share data from 1926 to date for their industrial, railroad, utility, and composite stock averages. For these same series, quarterly unadjusted and seasonally adjusted earnings per share are available dating from 1935. The data are published in Standard & Poor's *Trade and Securities Statistics Manual.* Earnings per share are generally taken as reported by the company and are comparable to the company figures in Standard & Poor's *Corporation Records.*

An even more useful and analytical tool is Standard & Poor's *Analysts Handbook,* which provides composite balance sheet and income account items constructed in such a way as to maintain maximum continuity over the years and to relate these items directly to the identical stock groups for which price indexes are available.

The items reported, all in terms of a constant unit of stock, are: sales, operating profit, depreciation, Federal income taxes, capital expenditures, book value, working capital, earnings, and dividends — all related to stock prices. In addition to the above, six significant ratios are included: profit margins, earnings as a percentage of sales, dividend-payout ratios, percentage return on book value, price-earnings ratios, and dividend yields.

All of these items are available for the period 1946 to date for some 84 individual industrial groups in addition to a composite of 425 industrial stocks. On the whole, the group series have fairly good continuity, enabling the analyst to compare company performance over the years with these composite measures. Where substitutions or a radical change in a company's activity affects the group composite, it is noted on the tables.

Most of the items in the *Handbook* are reported annually only. A monthly supplement is published which updates sales, taxes, earnings, and dividends, on a quarterly basis, with the same ratios based on the available items that appear in the *Handbook*. The monthly supplements also report Standard & Poor's estimates of composite per share earnings, by groups, for the current year; these estimates are revised every month. Current dividend yields also are shown, based on the latest indicated payment and the latest stock-price index.

Moody's. Moody's also publishes annual aggregates of sales and earnings for 50 individual industries based on data from 357 companies. The data are available by year from 1947 to date. Similar figures are also available for a total of 452 industrial companies, Class I railroads, the airline industry, and electric, telephone, telegraph, and gas utilities. These figures are published in the Moody's manuals, so they are not available until the manuals are.

SELECTING THE SUITABLE PROFIT SERIES

Having described the profit series generally available, I can now consider their suitability for the various needs of the economist, the businessman, and the financial analyst.

General Analysis. For analysis of savings, capital spending, and other trends in the national economy, the national income series of the Department of Commerce is most useful. Conceptually, this series fits into the framework of the national income accounts and therefore can be used as part of an examination of the economy of the United States. The utility of the series has been considerably enhanced in recent years since the Department of Commerce has provided quarterly data on corporate gross product and its components that can be related to past records and future estimates of gross national product.[5]

For estimating revenue of the federal government, projections of future income tax receipts are required. Estimates of corporate income tax returns can be based on the close relation between the tax returns and the figures for corporate profits prepared by the Department of Commerce.

Cyclical Turns. Because of their unusual sensitivity to changing economic conditions, corporate profits have been designated a leading indicator of cyclical turning points by the National Bureau of Economic Research, and the quarterly series of the Department of Commerce is ordinarily used by most economists in appraising current profit trends. However, this profits series is subject to wide errors in preliminary estimates until the income tax data on which it is based finally become available to the Department of Commerce about two years after the year for which profits are reported. A study by the Office of Statistical Standards in February 1960 [6] indicated that, for the period 1947–1958, the first estimate of corporate profits before taxes missed changes in direction nine times, or 19 per cent of the time; four of these nine times were at cyclical turning points. In addition, if the differences between the first and last estimates for each calendar quarter from 1947 to 1958 are totaled and averaged, this average is 40 per cent of the average of the differences between the successive quarterly profit figures finally reported. A further analysis of mine revealed that, in twenty of the forty-eight calendar quarters from 1947 to 1958, revised estimates subsequent to the first estimate were further away from the final figures than the first estimate was. Changes in seasonal corrections are partly responsible for the quarterly revisions.

Compilers of this profit series should not be censured for these errors in early estimates. Considering the nature of the material available, one must admit it is remarkable that the compilers do as well as they do. The Office of Business Economics has frequently stressed the need for

[5] See Robert E. Graham, Jr., and Jacqueline Bouman, "Corporate Profits and National Output," *Survey of Current Business*, XLII, No. 11 (November 1962), 19–27.

[6] *Revision of First Estimates of Quarter-to-Quarter Movement in Selected National Income Series, 1947–58 (Seasonally Adjusted Data), Statistical Evaluation Reports No. 2,* Office of Statistical Standards, Bureau of the Budget, Executive Office of the President (Washington, D.C.: Bureau of the Budget, February 1960).

better data on which to base estimates for the non-manufacturing sector. Further exploration of the growing differences between profits reported to shareholders and those reported for tax purposes would seem necessary also. It appears reasonable to say, however, that only the most tentative conclusions about movements of corporate profits can be based on the early quarterly estimates of profits by the Department of Commerce since actual movement is not known until two years or more after the fact. It is not surprising, therefore, that one of the leading proponents of the statistical indicator school should give corporate profits little weight in his current appraisals of business conditions.[7]

A considerable number of workers have explored the cyclical characteristics of the series of the First National City Bank[8] to ascertain its suitability as an indicator of cyclical turning points. The National Bureau of Economic Research has found that one of the series with fairly consistent leads at cyclical turning points is a computation of the percentage of the total number of companies with profits higher than those of the preceding quarter, the total of the percentages being seasonally adjusted. *Business Cycle Developments*, published by the Bureau of the Census, reports this series currently, as does the First National City Bank. For the analysis of current developments in the business cycle, this series would seem more useful than the somewhat less certain profit series of the Office of Business Economics.

An additional sensitive indicator of profit trends in the manufacturing sector is provided by the time series published monthly in *Business Cycle Developments*. This series, designated a leading indicator of cyclical turning points in business by the National Bureau of Economic Research, is called the price per unit of labor cost index. It is computed by taking a ratio of an index of wholesale prices of manufactured goods to an index of compensation of employees (sum of wages, salaries, and supplements to wages and salaries) per unit of output. The labor cost per unit of output takes into account both hourly compensation and output per man hour. The series is seasonally adjusted. Inasmuch as it relates prices to labor costs (one of the most important

[7] See Leonard H. Lempert, "Corporate Profits as a Contemporary Business Indicator," *Proceedings of Business and Economic Statistics Section, 1961* (Washington, D.C.: American Statistical Association), pp. 225–229.

[8] Geoffrey Moore, *Business Cycle Indicators* (New York: National Bureau of Economic Research, 1961), Vol. I, Ch. 11–12, especially pp. 345ff.

elements of cost), the index is, in effect, an implicit measure of profit margins. The lead of this series at cyclical turning points has, on the average, been longer than the lead of corporate profits themselves. The series is also of considerable value in following trends in the margin of profit.[9]

Industrial and Financial Analysis. The businessman and the financial analyst are interested in comparisons of profits for companies, industries, and sometimes broader aggregates, but their essential concern lies in the analysis of profits reported to shareholders. Therefore, the series of the Federal Reserve Board, that of the First National City Bank, and that of the FTC–SEC are most helpful.

The series of the Federal Reserve Board provides a measure of the results of a consistent sample of shareholder reports for six large manufacturing groups as well as for three regulated industries and the banking industry. Information includes sales, profits before and after taxes, and dividends. However, the groupings may be too broad for detailed analysis of industries, and only large companies are included in the manufacturing sector.

The series of the First National City Bank provides the greatest detail about industries; in the annual review, some sixty-five separate industrial categories are analyzed. Moreover, this series provides information not readily available elsewhere about the non-manufacturing sector. Unfortunately, the information is restricted to net income and the percentage of changes in income from the previous year, rate of return on sales, and rate of return on net assets. Nevertheless, for measuring broad trends in profits, the series of the First National City Bank is one of the most useful.

In the manufacturing sector, the series of the FTC–SEC provides the greatest wealth of information for comparison. Thirty-one industrial classifications are covered, as well as nine classifications by asset size — but, unfortunately, no cross-classification. Financial data include detailed income accounts and balance sheets. In addition, rates of change in sales and profits, profits per dollar of sales, annual rates of profit on stockholders' equity, and financial statements in ratio form are provided. This series is one of the most useful tools for historical analysis.

[9] For a further discussion and description of this series, see *Tested Knowledge of Business Cycles,* 42nd Annual Report, National Bureau of Economic Research (New York, June 1962), pp. 9–15. See also Edgar R. Fiedler, "Keeping Posted on Profits," *Financial Analysts Journal,* XX, No. 3 (May–June 1964), 50–51.

CONCLUSION

To restate briefly the points made in this paper, reports of profit can be broadly divided into those to shareholders, those for taxes, and those for the national income accounts. Statistically and conceptually, these profit series are different.

For purposes of general economic analysis, the national income series of the Department of Commerce generally provides the most useful information. For the businessman or the financial analyst, the series of the First National City Bank and of the FTC–SEC in the manufacturing sector are recommended.

The most important thing, however, is the need for better understanding and discrimination by the specific users of various measures of profits. This greater care is essential for better analyses of trends in profits and for intelligent presentation of information about profits to the general public.

Comments   **FREDERICK L. DEMING**

EDMUND A. MENNIS's paper about measuring corporate profit is an excellent presentation of different concepts and measurements of profits. I regard it as a valuable addition to the record. It provides calm, objective, and useful perspectives on measurement of profits. Almost explicitly, certainly implicitly, Dr. Mennis points out that precise measurement of profits is most difficult and that, in a sense, profits are what management, law, and varying accounting conventions say they are. His discussion and brief analysis of the several sources of information about profits and the various time series relating to profits are well done and are both interesting and informative.

I realize that it is decidedly inappropriate for a discussant to give unstinted praise to a paper, but I find nothing to criticize in Dr. Mennis's paper and can express nothing but admiration for a very good piece of work.

+ + +   EDMUND A. MENNIS

The Outlook for Corporate Profits

AN EVALUATION of the outlook for corporate profits in the United States may be conveniently divided into the following sections: (1) a review of the postwar record for profits in order to obtain a better perspective of the present position of profits; (2) an examination of trends in demand, costs, and prices, which are major determinants of profits; (3) the selection of an appropriate measure as a basis for projecting profits; and (4) the outlook for profits as viewed in May 1964.

THE POSTWAR RECORD FOR PROFITS

If we examine the statistics of after-tax corporate profits in the postwar period, the performance has been disappointing.[1] As Henry Ford II has pointed out, after-tax profits in 1963 were $27 billion, not significantly better than the $23.5 billion in 1956, the $23 billion in 1950, and the $20.5 billion as long ago as 1948. As a percentage of gross national product, corporate profits in 1963 were 4.6 per cent, compared with 5.8 per cent in 1955 and 8 per cent in 1950. To put it in another way, since 1950, profits have increased by less than 20 per cent, whereas gross national product has increased 106 per cent, employee compensation 120 per cent, governmental spending 179 per cent, and prices 33 per cent. In relative terms, profits have suffered a sharp decline. However, if the postwar period is examined in a somewhat different

[1] The statistical relationships described in this section were based on the latest national income account data available in May 1964. However, a substantial revision in the data was made in August 1965. Although the relationships were moderately changed by the revisions, the conclusions about profit trends would not be altered.

perspective, the performance of profits appears more satisfactory than the statistics just cited would indicate.

Rate of Return on Capital. A traditional measure of profitability is the rate of return on capital invested. Although no completely satisfactory historical series of the rate of return for all corporations is available, the First National City Bank does provide such a measure for the companies for which it has maintained records from 1925 to date.

If this series is examined, a decline in the postwar rate of return is clearly evident. For manufacturing companies, the rate of return fell from 18.9 per cent in 1948 to 9.9 per cent in 1961 and returned only to 11.5 per cent in 1963. For industry generally, the rate of return fell from 14 per cent in 1948 to 8.7 per cent in 1961 and improved only to 9.5 per cent in 1963. However, if the figures for rate of return are reviewed in the broader perspective of the period 1925–1963, the 1948–1950 period represents the highest rates of return in that long span of thirty-nine years. The very high rates of return in the years immediately after World War II contrast sharply with the very low rates of return in the period 1930–1935 (less than 5 per cent). In general, the rate of return seems to fluctuate around 10 per cent, about where it is in 1964. This raises the question of whether anything unusual in the immediate postwar period made those years a poor base against which to compare recent performance.

Inventory Profits. Two unusual factors may explain the very high level of profits, both absolutely and relatively, in the immediate postwar period. Because of the rapid rise in prices after World War II, corporations experienced an unusually high level of inventory profits, which, in effect, overstated reported profits. For example, inventory profits for 1946 have been estimated by the Department of Commerce at $5.3 billion, or 23 per cent of profits before taxes as reported by the Department of Commerce; for 1947, this figure is $5.9 billion, or 20 per cent; and for 1950, $5.0 billion, or 12 per cent.

Depreciation. A second unusual factor inflated profit figures in the years just after World War II. During the war, plant and equipment expenditures were low. Consequently, in the immediate postwar years, plant and equipment were both old and well depreciated, and the costs of replacing them were rising. A new plant had to be built, but depreciation allowances were completely inadequate to replace the old plant. This under-depreciation recorded in corporate accounts resulted in a further overstatement of the profit level. As Richard Holton has described in his paper in this book, the Department of Commerce has prepared estimates of postwar corporate depreciation assuming a straight-line replacement-cost basis of accounting, which can be compared with the depreciation actually taken on tax reports. The depreciation understatement in the period 1947–1949 was about $3.5 billion, or between 41 and 45 per cent of the actual depreciation taken on the books for corporate tax purposes.

Drawing on the work of the Department of Commerce, we can therefore compare reported domestic corporate profits after taxes with profits as adjusted for these inventory profits and for under-depreciation. As reported, domestic corporate profits after taxes from 1947 to 1963 increased from $17.6 billion to $24.4 billion, a gain of 38 per cent. However, after adjustment for these two factors, domestic corporate profits after taxes increased from $8.9 billion to $24.4 billion during this period, a gain of 174 per cent. Consequently, if allowance is made for these two factors, the performance of profits certainly looks better. To rephrase it, the quality of current profits has improved recently compared with the immediate postwar years because there are no substantial inventory profits, owing to rising prices, and because depreciation allowances are more realistic, owing to substantially revised laws and codes concerning depreciation.

An alternative way to examine trends in profit would be to look at corporate profits *before* taxes and depreciation and *after* adjustment for inventory profits, taking the resulting figure as a percentage of gross national product. For the period 1947–1963, this figure has consistently ranged around 15 per cent, with a slight drift down from 1955 through 1961 and a slight rise since 1961. This evidence further supports the thesis that the principal causes of the decline in profits from the 1948–1950 peaks were inadequate depreciation and inventory profits in the base period.

DEMAND, COSTS, AND PRICES

More important than the historical record of profits to date, however, is the question of the outlook for profits in the years ahead. Assumptions about the future of profits can be made more intelligently if we examine the trends in the three major determinants of profits: demand, costs, and prices.

Demand. With respect to demand, the period since 1947 may be divided into three broad periods, and a hasty sketch of these periods can be filled in by the reader's own recollections and experience. From 1947 to 1955–1957, consumer and corporate demand represented essentially the satisfying of shortages that resulted from World War II. Both consumers and businesses came out of the war with substantial liquid assets and a definite shortage of goods. For the next ten years or so, this pent-up demand was being satisfied, particularly for durables such as automobiles, homes, appliances, and plant and equipment. These ten years were also a period of labor shortages and of rising costs that could be passed on by rising prices. The period was extended by the Korean war (1950–1953). The postwar era really ended in the booming sale of automobiles and housing in 1955, although the boom in capital goods did not end until two years later, 1957.

The period from 1955–1957 to 1961 might be considered one of digestion and adjustment. The consumer was now well stocked with goods; overcapacity existed in many industries; costs continued to rise in the early part of the period; intense competition and a restrictive monetary policy flattened out the price trend; profits were under increasing pressure.

The third period, in which we find ourselves in 1964, may be dated from 1961. Although we cannot characterize it properly yet, it seems a period of more balanced, normal growth. In any event, it appears to be markedly different from the previous two periods, since it lacks both the excess of demand characteristic of 1947–1955 and the excess of capacity characteristic of 1955–1961.

The differences in these three periods can be illustrated most effectively by examining two areas in durable goods. Sales of automobiles expanded rapidly from 3.0 million cars in 1947 to 7.4 million in 1955, which was well above any "normal" demand at that time. For 1956–1961, automobile sales sagged noticeably. Since 1961, however, a series of successive new highs in sales have been reported. More importantly, the automobile companies have estimated that current sales levels are much closer to a sustainable rate than they were a decade ago. In capital goods, outlays by business rose from $20 billion in 1947 to $37 billion in 1957, declined sharply in 1958, and reached the 1957 level again only in 1962. Capital expenditures were 7–8 per cent of gross national product in 1949–1955, reached a high of 8.5 per cent in 1956–1957, and have stayed under 7 per cent since 1958. In 1961, this percentage began to improve, and in 1964 it will once again be close to 7 per cent. Moreover, there are some indications that higher levels of spending for plant and equipment lie ahead. Internally generated funds are higher; operating rates are closer to capacity; and competition at home and abroad forces better cost control and development of new products.

The favorable prospects for demand in these two important areas therefore suggest that, from the side of demand at least, the current period of economic activity is different from that from 1955–1957 to 1961.

Costs. In addition to greater demand, two other significant forces are affecting profits favorably in 1964. They are unit labor costs and prices.

The figure for unit labor costs is a combination of employee compensation per hour, including fringe benefits, and output per man hour, commonly called "productivity." The pattern of the combination — that is, the labor cost per unit of output — significantly affects trends in profit for the vital manufacturing sector of the economy. As is well known, hourly labor costs have risen fairly steadily since World War II. Productivity also has generally increased; although it slowed noticeably during the Korean war, it has seemed to be accelerating since 1961. Combining these two factors reveals that labor cost per unit of output rose consistently through 1957–1958 because hourly labor costs rose faster than productivity. For 1957–1961, unit labor costs were relatively flat, and they have actually been declining since 1961, reflecting in large part the substantial capital investment by business in new and modern facilities. Whether this favorable trend in unit labor costs continues will depend substantially on labor negotiations later in 1964, particularly in major industries such as production of automobiles. If future increases in costs of labor are approximately in line with improvements in productivity, the effect on profits will be favorable.

Prices. The trend in the manufacturing sector with respect to prices is well known. Prices rose fairly sharply after World War II, particularly during 1950–1951. The trend from 1951 to 1955 was relatively flat, but a further increase came between mid-1955 and mid-1958. The period since 1958 has been marked by general price stability in the manufacturing sector. In fact, the 1961 business recovery was unusual in that there were actually some moderate declines in prices, in contrast to the increases normally experienced in the expansion period follow-ing a business trough. Since 1963, prices have been somewhat more favorable for profits, with modest, although fairly widespread, in-creases. Whether or not this trend will continue depends upon competitive forces, the outcome of labor negotiations, and, possibly, political pressure, but, as a general statement, one can say that the downward pressure on prices seems to have stopped, and prices have improved somewhat.

As a result of the combination of lower unit labor costs and a some-what better price structure, profit margins in 1963 and thus far in 1964 have shown a marked improvement, reaching levels that compare very favorably with those reached in 1955, 1957, and 1959. (As I mention in my other paper in this book, current trends in profit margins can be followed in the monthly publication of the Department of Commerce, *Business Cycle Developments*, where it is shown as Series 17, the price per unit of labor cost index.)

A SUGGESTED PROFITS MEASURE

The next question is, How can these developments affecting profits be translated into assumptions about trends in future profits? In an earlier chapter, I have described the limitations of many of the profit series currently available. Because of the limitations of many of these series, the Wellington Management Company has devised its own survey of profits to provide some method of projecting future profits and con-trasting them with past ones.

Since early 1957, the research staff of Wellington Management Com-pany has been collecting and analyzing financial data for a representa-tive group of large companies in order to obtain a better idea of the outlook for these companies and their respective industries. The group covers 127 companies in 27 industries. These are large, successful com-panies, selected because of their suitability for investment. All of these companies except banks, insurance companies, and one manufacturing company are listed on the New York Stock Exchange. The total mar-ket value of the listed common stocks accounts for over half of the market value of all stocks listed on the Exchange.

The second reason these companies were selected was that the re-search staff of the Wellington Management Company knows their operations. Most of the companies are visited periodically by the staff, and Wellington has extensive files about their past not only from the usual financial sources, but also, in many instances, from confidential sources as well. Although relatively few in number, these companies, with aggregate net income reported to shareholders of about $15 billion, account for a substantial portion of aggregate profits in this country.

Profit reports for this group of companies have been compiled and analyzed for the postwar period. In addition, estimates of future profits for each of the companies are gathered and tabulated by industry each quarter. The senior security analyst responsible for each industry prepares estimates based on the industrial analyses, field visits (including discussions with corporate officials), and the general economic analyses made by the staff at Wellington and by consultants. All estimates are prepared in the light of current assumptions about business made by Wellington, so that a report can be internally consistent.

As a further analytical technique, it is helpful to divide these industries into three separate categories. The first includes "basic" industries — such major industries as those producing automobiles, steels, metals, oils, chemicals, and machinery. The second category covers "growth" industries — firms dealing in office equipment, drugs, and electronics and a miscellaneous selection of growth companies. The third category, called "combination" (because it combines somewhat slower, but steadier, growth and some current yield), consists principally of service industries, such as electric utilities and telephone, insurance, and merchandising companies.

POSTWAR PROFITS PERFORMANCE

The average annual increase in earnings per share of these industries in the postwar period is shown in the accompanying table. Several facts are interesting. The average annual increase in earnings per share for all companies for the period was 6.7 per cent. The pattern of increase, however, is not uniform, with the least growth (0.8 per cent per year) occurring in the 1955–1961 period. As the industry categories in the last three columns indicate, this slowing of the gain in earnings was concentrated in basic industries, where an actual decrease in earnings at an annual rate of 2 per cent per year occurred from 1955 to 1961. Since 1961, a resumption of much more rapid increases in earnings in the basic industries has been evident and, for the reasons discussed, a better outlook for profit in this area may occur in the years immediately ahead.

Properly, of course, the point should be made that profits, particularly in the basic industries, are subject to cyclical influences, and the period since early 1961 has been one of cyclical expansion in business. Consequently, the rather high rate of increase in profits, particularly in basic industries, probably will not be sustained. Even if this point is conceded, the evidence presented still raises the issue of whether forces affecting profits exist that transcend cyclical fluctuations and whether these forces, which so adversely affected reported profits in the 1955–

Increases in Earnings per Share for Selected Companies, 1947–1964

Period	All Companies	Basic Industries	Growth Industries	Combination Industries
1947–1955	9.9%	11.6%	8.0%	5.7%
1955–1961	0.8	−2.0	12.0	5.8
1961–1964[a]	10.9	13.7	11.2	5.1
1947–1964[a]	6.7	6.9	10.0	5.7

[a] Estimate.

1961 period, have changed. Although it is not argued that profits will continue to grow at the rate of 11 per cent they grew in 1961 through my estimate for 1964, it is suggested that the so-called "profits squeeze" of the latter part of the 1950's may be behind us.

Outlook for 1964. With respect to 1964, it may be of interest to summarize the results of the most recent survey of profits by Wellington. The assumptions about business used as a basis for the estimates of profits were built around an assumed gross national product of $623 billion and an industrial production index of 131.

The increases in earnings per share for 1964 versus 1963 for all of the companies in the survey and for each of the three major components were as follows: for all companies, 11.6 per cent; for basic industries, 13.0 per cent; for growth industries, 12.5 per cent; and for combination industries, 4.9 per cent. These figures represent estimates of earnings per share as reported to shareholders. Wellington also prepared estimates of 1964 profits to be reported by the Department of Commerce as a part of the national income accounts. These estimates are based on the assumption of a gross national product for 1964 of

$623 billion and use as an analytical framework the quarterly data on corporate gross product provided by the Department of Commerce. Most critical in the estimate of profits are the assumptions about costs of labor related to income originating in the corporate sector of the economy; the decline in this ratio provides the basis for the favorable profit results expected in 1964. Of course, in this series, as in the shareholder profits series, one reason for the predicted gain in profits in 1964 is the reduction of 2 per cent in the corporate income tax rate, which, other things being equal, makes profits after taxes higher than they otherwise would have been in the absence of a tax reduction. Specific estimates of the 1964 figures of the Department of Commerce are as follows: for corporate profits before taxes, $57.0 billion, an increase of 11.1 per cent over 1963; for corporate profits after taxes, $31.4 billion, an increase of 17.6 per cent over 1963.[2]

SUMMARY

Postwar profits trends, if an allowance is made for the inflated profits in the early postwar years, have been relatively satisfactory. A better perspective of profits can be gained if the postwar period is divided into three parts: the postwar boom; the period of adjustment; and the period of more balanced growth since 1961. In the early months of 1964, profits have been favorably affected by renewed growth in demand, especially for durable goods, better cost control, and some improvement in prices. A significant gain in earnings is expected for the whole of 1964. For the period beyond, although cyclical influences will still affect profit trends, one can hope that the profit squeeze of the late 1950's remains behind us.

[2] Before the revisions in the national income accounts mentioned in footnote 1 (p. 50), the actual profits reported for 1964 were $57.6 billion and $31.8 billion.

PROFITS IN THE FIRM + + +

Editors' Introduction

THE attention of theoreticians in recent years has increasingly been centered on decision-making in the individual business firm. It is understandable that profits — the carrot in the enterprise process — provide a common focal point for analysts and theoreticians of various disciplines. "True" profits are, of course, not determinable for a firm because of all the changes in products, factors of production, and prices in the real world. The question, then, is whether accountants are measuring and presenting a profit appropriate to its users. The papers and discussions of this section are concerned with this question and present the measurements of profit and viewpoints of economists, accountants, and financial analysts about the use of profit.

What the accountant measures and labels "profit" must serve for diverse uses. The seemingly confused state of measurements of profit is succinctly described by Joel Segall's comment that we don't know what we measure and accountants measure it badly.

Myron Gordon presents an economist's viewpoint of profit measurement and chastises accountants for their belief that Hicks's definition of income[1] is theoretically superior to the cost definition employed by accountants. That definition would be useful only where the future is certain and the individual has infinite life. He suggests that the various distributions from income be recognized and that retained income be treated as benefiting all parties with rights in the corporation.

Carl Nelson is critical of his profession of accounting, commenting

[1] In which a man's income is the maximum value which he can consume during a week and still expect to be as well off at the end of the week as he was at the beginning.

Profits in the Modern Economy

that methods of processing data in the large corporation are little changed from those in a one-man shop. He believes what deters good profit measurement is that we do not explicitly know what we want to measure. He offers three possible approaches for accountants: develop an income concept both economically significant and operational, measure income consistently but without economic significance, or abandon the idea of measuring income and substitute other information.

Pearson Hunt, discussing the financial analyst's viewpoint, stresses the meaning of profits to the stockholders of the firm and suggests that their concern for dividends points up the necessity for the firm to show sufficient internal cash flows as well as earnings per share.

The cash-flow concept of profits is further suggested by Joel Segall. He believes that managerial performance and profitability should be evaluated by net cash flows to stockholders, including changes in the value of stock. This analysis is more thoroughly explored in the paper by Diran Bodenhorn, who believes it desirable to have a profit concept which can be measured on the basis of market values so that the measurement will be objective in the accounting sense. Francis Boddy suggests that knowledge of the tax position and interests of stockholders of a particular concern could help managers and investors to view profits as success indicators.

The use of profit figures in capital investment decisions in the business firm is the center of attention for several papers. Harold Bierman, Jr., reviews the principal methods used to analyze investment decisions and concludes that a firm can institute procedures to improve the decision-making process and benefit the stockholders and the economy. J. Fred Weston focuses on the sources of funds and costs of obtaining them and shows how the optimal financial mix can contribute to the profitability of the firm. He brings together numerous theoretical and environmental threads to show how financial policies and decisions can contribute to an increase in the profitability of the firm. Daniel Holland cites the findings of a study he and Paul Cootner undertook to determine what relation there is between risk and the rates of return experienced by firms. Businessmen are seen to be motivated by the return they think they can earn on their assets; the expected value for their decisions is the possible monetary returns weighted by both their utility and their probability of occurrence. The riskier the firm, the higher its profit rate.

MYRON J. GORDON

An Economist's View of Profit Measurement

BACK in 1939 the famous economist J. R. Hicks defined a man's income as "the maximum value which he can consume during a week, and still expect to be as well off at the end of the week as he was at the beginning." [1] In 1950 another distinguished economist, Sidney Alexander, proposed this definition of income as a basis for the measurement of corporate profits and used it to evaluate critically the definition of cost employed by accountants. [2] Accountants for the most part have since accepted the theoretical validity of the Hicks-Alexander, or, as it has come to be called, the economist's definition. Some have defended the accounting approach to profit measurement on the grounds that it is practical, whereas others have proposed modifications in the direction of making it a closer approximation of the Hicks-Alexander definition.

Economists, among others, customarily look on what accountants do and say as wrong, and since I am playing the role of the economist in this paper, I too must take that position. However, what I shall try to show is that the accountant is wrong in accepting the theoretical superiority of the economist's definition of income. On theoretical as well as practical grounds, cost is superior to the present value concept that emerges from the economist's definition of income. Economists love to argue; if we can't fight with someone else, we'll argue among ourselves.

My paper may be summarized briefly as follows. The Hicks-Alex-

---

[1] J. R. Hicks, *Value and Capital* (Oxford: Clarendon, 1939), p. 172.

[2] Sidney S. Alexander, "Income Measurement in a Dynamic Economy," *Five Monographs on Business Income* (New York: American Institute of Accountants, July 1, 1950). A revision in collaboration with David Solomons appears in W. T. Baxter and Sidney Davidson, eds., *Studies in Accounting Theory* (Homewood, Ill.: Irwin, 1962).

ander definition of income may be useful for a person faced with the decision of how much to spend or consume during the current period and not consume in future periods. However, this definition is useful only under the assumptions that the future is certain and that the individual has an infinite life — neither of which is true (though the latter is a fair approximation for the large modern corporation). When these assumptions are withdrawn, the Hicks-Alexander definition is of no use even for making consumption and dividend decisions.

I shall not in this paper consider the measurement of income or profit for consumption and dividend decisions. Lintner,[3] Friedman,[4] Ando and Modigliani,[5] and I,[6] among others, have done work in this area. There are other purposes for which one may want to know the income of a person or corporation. In particular, one may want to know how efficiently the person or corporation used the resources at his command during a period. How much did he produce? In a world where the management of resources is delegated to others and the consequences of their and our decisions are only partially revealed — and then only with the passage of time — the problem of performance evaluation is far more important than are dividend decisions. The appropriate definition of income for this purpose has its foundation in the accountant's and not the economist's approach to the subject. Specifically, it will be argued that current cost is the best conceptual basis of income measurement for the purpose of providing information for evaluation of performance. It will also be noted that, given the manner in which accounting principles are being manipulated to provide management with the income figure it wants to report, cash flows may prove to be a better measure of income for evaluation of performance than is the figure the accountant is persuaded to label "income." Finally, some comments will be made on the relevance of measuring profit for decision-making.

What is the Hicks-Alexander definition of income? Assume there is an individual who has an infinite life, has $100,000, and can lend or

[3] John Lintner, "Distribution of Incomes of Corporations among Dividends, Retained Earnings and Taxes," *American Economic Review*, XLVI (May 1956), 97–113.

[4] Milton Friedman, *A Theory of the Consumption Function* (Princeton: Princeton University Press, 1957).

[5] Albert Ando and Franco Modigliani, "The 'Life Cycle' Hypothesis of Saving," *American Economic Review*, LIII (May 1963), 55–84.

[6] Myron J. Gordon, *The Investment, Financing and Valuation of the Corporation* (Homewood, Ill.: Irwin, 1962).

borrow freely at 5 per cent with certainty. The $100,000 is equivalent to an annuity in perpetuity of $5,000 per year. Capital and income are but two sides of the same coin under certainty. The individual may spend $5,000 in the current period and still be as well off at the end of the period as he was at the start. Therefore, the income for the period is $5,000. He may decide to spend less than $5,000 during the current period and more in one or more future periods. However, the information that the income for the period is $5,000 will help him in making his decision about consumption.

Now assume that the individual will live just three years. We may say that his income is still $5,000, meaning this time that if he spends $5,000 his wealth will remain unchanged. However, he is not so well off at the end of the period as he was at the start. His remaining life has been reduced from three to two years. You may believe that this objection to the Hicks-Alexander definition of income gives it a meaning that was not intended by its authors. Perhaps you are right. But perhaps they should not have used the term "as well off." What they should have said is that income is the goods and services one may consume and still have the same capital at the end as at the start of a period.

What happens when the assumption that the future is certain is withdrawn? The individual now has a block of shares in a corporation that has a current market value of $50,000 and that he expects will pay a dividend of $5,000 per year in perpetuity. Assume, however, that during the year a dividend of only $3,000 is paid. Also, at the end of the year the market value of the stock falls to $37,500, and the future dividends he can expect are $3,000 per year in perpetuity. What is his income for the year? How much could he spend and be as well off at the end as at the start of the year? One possible Hicks-Alexander figure is the $3,000 dividend minus the $12,500 fall in the value of the stock or a loss of $9,500. Another Hicks-Alexander solution is obtained as follows. The return on the stock has gone down from 10 to 8 per cent. To raise the expected future dividends from $3,000 back to $5,000 the investment in the stock must be raised to $62,500. His income therefore is $3,000 minus the $25,000 needed to raise the investment in the stock to the level that will provide an expected $5,000 per period.

I do not wish to argue the relative merits of these two alternatives.[7]

[7] See David Solomons, "Economic and Accounting Concepts of Income," *Accounting Review*, XXXVI, No. 3 (July 1961), 374–383.

Profits in the Modern Economy

The point is that, broadly speaking, under both income is the cash receipt during a period plus or minus the present value of the change in expected future cash receipts. Under uncertainty, the income realized in a single period is determined for the most part by the change in one's expectation with respect to subsequent periods. Some may consider this definition of income bizarre; others may consider it clever. The relevant question, however, is, How useful is it?

Recall that the problem for which the individual may be interested in knowing his income is his decision about consumption. The individual knows what dividend he received during the period, and he knows the value of the stock and his expected future dividends at the start and the end of the period. How is he aided in making an optimal decision about consumption for the period by learning that his income in the last period was a loss of $9,500? An individual who believes firmly that he should spend only his income would have an extremely difficult time. Fortunately, most people are more flexible. They go about making their decisions on consumption in a different way.

Before proceeding, I should like to point out that what I have just said disagrees little, if at all, with Professor Hicks's position on the subject. Before he presented the definition I quoted above, Hicks said, "The purpose of income calculations in practical affairs is to give people an indication of the amount which they can consume without impoverishing themselves." [8] I agree that is the purpose the Hicks definition serves, if it serves any purpose. There is a more important area of agreement. In *Value and Capital*, Hicks developed a dynamic theory of the price, production, consumption, and other economic decisions that individuals and firms make. On the relation between income and his theory in these areas, he wrote, "we have refrained from using the term income in our dynamic theory." [9] He explained that the definition did not have the logical precision he required and that he found it unnecessary to use the concept.

A different and perhaps more important reason for establishing the income or profit of a company is to obtain information for the management of the resources under the control of the company. In an ideal world the owner or manager of a company would consider all the alternative courses of action open to him within the framework of a model

[8] Hicks, *Value and Capital*, p. 172.
[9] *Ibid.*

66

or theory that might be used to arrive at the optimal decision or sequence of decisions over time. In this ideal world, there would be no
need to look back and question the decision-makers' performance. The
circumstances which govern the alternatives open to the firm would be
completely known, and the model itself would be a perfect decision-
making entity. One would need only to program the model in a computer; the outcomes would be the best possible, regardless of how good
or bad they proved to be. The owner or manager would be just a
figurehead.

This ideal world — an abstraction bearing little resemblance to reality
— often blinds us to reality. In fact, the environment of a firm and
the alternatives open to its manager are imperfectly known. The extent
and accuracy with which the environment and alternative possible
courses of action are perceived will depend in large measure on the
effort and ability of the manager to see through the fog. Further, the
criteria of choice and the decision-making process are a strange mixture
of rules of thumb, sub-optimizing models, and intuition. Psychologists
may provide a more accurate description of the decision-making process than does traditional economic theory. There is some very interesting research attempting to synthesize the behavioralists' and the economists' image of decision-making in the firm.[10]

One aspect of the picture that emerges may be summarized as follows: A manager develops an approach to his responsibility. He himself may be called a decision-making model — one that is partly rational,
partly rule of thumb, and partly intuitive, as stated earlier. However,
the manager periodically looks back to see how he has been doing. If
he believes he has been successful, the elements of his decision-making
process are reinforced. He may change and innovate, but cautiously
and on a small scale. He will not seriously question his basic view of
the world and his rules of decision. On the other hand, if he has not been
successful, he will look more carefully at his environment to discover
what, if anything, has escaped his notice. More important, he will question his mode of behavior or decision-making rules. He will search for
and be receptive to new objectives and criteria of choice.

An analogous picture may be drawn for the stockholder who has
delegated the management of his property to the officers of the corpo-

[10] For example, see Richard M. Cyert and James G. March, *A Behavioral Theory of the Firm* (Englewood Cliffs, N.J.: Prentice-Hall, 1963).

ration and for the superior who has delegated authority to subordinates. If those delegated do well, the stockholder's confidence in them is strengthened, and if they don't do well, he questions their ability and considers the desirability of finding a new management.

Our objective, then, is the measurement of income in a manner that is most informative about how well the manager of an economic unit has been doing. That is, How efficiently has he been employing the resources of his firm? What I now propose to show is that current cost — not the so-called economist's present value or the traditional accountant's historical cost basis of valuation — provides the best measure of income for this purpose.

For simplicity, let us begin by considering a farmer whose only asset is his land, which is not subject to depreciation. We could all agree that the value of his crop less the labor and material employed to produce the crop is the correct definition of his income. Changes in the prices of farm products and other events will change the value of the land, but few would argue that the capital gains or losses that result should be included in his annual income since doing so would only distort the income figure as a measure of his performance.

The value of a farmer's crop will change from one year to the next depending on what crops he plants, the supply of and demand for the crops, business conditions, acts of nature, and acts of Congress. Some of these determinants of his income may be looked on as being under his control and some as being beyond it. To separate the influence of events beyond his control from those within his control would be desirable for evaluating the changes in his income as a measure of his performance. In intra-company accounting, standard costs systems do this in some measure. However, if analysis of variances by cause on the level of the firm is impossible, the total actual income may still be useful as an indication of performance.

The advocates of the Hicks-Alexander definition of income may counter that the change in the value of the firm also provides information on the farmer's performance, and in a sense, they are right. However, the information is about the farmer's wisdom in becoming a farmer instead of investing his wealth in some other business. If one accepts his ownership of the farm and is concerned only with his performance during the year, the value of the crop is the relevant measure of income. Including capital gains or losses, realized or unrealized, in the income figure distorts its meaning.

Land is not the only asset of business enterprises and of farms. Depreciable assets, buildings and equipment, and inventories are also required to carry on business. The traditional and dominant practice in accounting is to define income of a period as sales revenue less the actual cost of the assets consumed to realize the revenue. This is the historical, or actual, cost principle. It originated with the seventeenth-century merchant for whom money was the only permanent form of wealth. He would buy whatever commodity could be resold for a profit at that time. Each purchase-sale transaction was a logical entity for this merchant, and the income on each such transaction or on all transactions consummated in a period was meaningful information.

Accountants have carried this concept into the twentieth century. An accountant's measure of the income of a modern corporation is sales revenue less the cost of the labor employed two to three months earlier, the material purchased three to nine months earlier, the equipment that may have been purchased about ten years earlier, and a building purchased up to thirty years earlier. Changes in the value of these assets between the period they are considered "purchased" and the period they are considered "sold" are included in the income of the latter period.

The fact of the matter, however, is that the turnover in these assets is more apparent than real. The inventory and plant of the modern corporation are fixed assets no less than is the land of the traditional farmer. For instance, the modern department store carries an inventory for the continuing profit to be obtained in retail merchandising and not for the profit to be obtained from selling the inventory. The conclusion which follows is that changes in the value of these assets are capital gains or losses and not elements of operating income. In other words, sales revenue less the current cost of the labor, material, and equipment consumed to obtain the revenue is the profit figure for a period that provides the most effective measure of the performance of a corporation during the period. The techniques for implementing current cost as a basis of valuation and a more detailed argument in support of it have been presented elsewhere.[11]

[11] See "The Valuation of Accounts at Current Cost," *Accounting Review*, XXVIII, No. 3 (July 1953), 373–384 (reprinted in Stephen Zeff and Thomas Keller, *Financial*

Profits in the Modern Economy

There are two other fundamental problems in measuring income so as to provide information about the performance of managers to their superiors. Since other papers in this collection take up these problems, I shall comment only briefly on them.

The first problem is the expenditures made in one period for the purpose of increasing profits in future periods — expenditures which nonetheless are charged as expenses against the sales revenue of the current period. Though this is an old problem, it deserves mention because it increases in importance every year. Expenditures on research and development, on plant modifications, on some types of sales promotion, and on strengthening the organization of the firm are undertaken in part or in total to increase income in future periods. They are not part of the costs or the expenses needed to obtain the sales revenue of the current period.

As the consequence of this practice, these expenditures that are actually investments are a means of manipulating the reported current income of profit. If revenue less the true expenses of the period is expected to be small, expenditures that are investments may be reduced to ameliorate or reduce the fall in reported income — and vice versa.

Accountants defend the recording of these expenditures as expenses on the grounds that they know no objective and true method of assigning lives to these types of assets and measuring their consumption over their lives. The fact of the matter is that any reasonable life and any reasonable method of amortization over the life, such as sum of digits, will result in an income statement that is more nearly true and more objective than the statement that results from current practice.

It appears that the accounting profession lacks the will or the power to limit the freedom of corporate managers to manipulate their reported income. What is worse, there appears to be no great concern about this state of affairs. A possible explanation is that our defense of private property has become so vigorous that we have forgotten why we support it. Private ownership may be superior to public ownership,

---

Accounting Theory (New York: McGraw-Hill, 1964)), for the techniques involved in using current cost as a basis of valuation. The argument for current cost and its role in performance evaluation are elaborated in "Scope and Method of Theory and Research in the Measurement of Income and Wealth," Accounting Review, XXXV, No. 4 (October 1960), 603–618, and in "Postulates, Principles and Research in Accounting," Accounting Review, XXXIX, No. 2 (April 1964), 251–263. For another view, see Edgar O. Edwards and Philip W. Bell, The Theory and Measurement of Business Income (Berkeley and Los Angeles: University of California Press, 1961).

because property can be administered more efficiently under the control of private owners than under the control of bureaucrats. However, the advantage of the private owner, the stockholder in the economy of today, over the government bureaucrat may not be so great that he will make better decisions than the bureaucrat when he does not have the information about the performance of his company needed to make intelligent decisions.

The principles of accounting are a sturdy set of tools, but they are deteriorating rapidly under the impact of the radical changes taking place in the nature of business operations. Principles that were satisfactory during the 1930's are no longer adequate today, and unless we begin bringing them up to date, we will soon reach a state of affairs in which the income and other data of financial statements produced with the tools of the 1930's will leave the reader of financial statements completely misinformed.

The deterioration of accounting principles as instruments for providing information about the status and performance of a business enterprise is most dramatically revealed when one turns to the liability section of the balance sheet. There has always been trouble in measuring the amount and changes in the assets of a corporation, but at least the amount of its liabilities was not open to question. This is no longer the case.

The second problem in income determination we shall discuss arises from the fact that the providers of capital for a corporation, owners and creditors, are no longer the only parties with rights in the corporation. It is now popular to say that the workers, the management, the government, and the consumers also have rights. However, these statements are not just public relations propaganda. Pension plans, stock-option plans, and the corporate income tax have become concrete enough to present the accountant with problems of measuring the rights of the workers, managers, and government, but the accounting profession has so far failed to recognize that anything new has taken place.

It is quite evident, for example, that corporations do not have a legal liability to employees for the pensions specified in corporate pension plans. Corporate contributions to their pension plan trust fund therefore vary from one year to the next with the profitability of the corporation. Accountants nonetheless treat these payments as expenses and deduct them in computing the profit of the corporation. Accountants

71

also look on the federal income tax as an expense. Consequently, the difference between the tax actually paid and what the tax would have been if taxable income agreed with reported income is considered an expense. However, the validity of the expense and the related liability for deferred income taxes are open to question.

It is possible that the only way out of the present dilemma in measuring corporate profits is the recognition of the following facts: First, the distributions out of income by a corporation include interest to creditors, pension plan payments to trust funds, the value of grants to officers, and income tax payments to governments, as well as dividends paid to owners. Second, income retained by a corporation benefits all with rights in the corporation, not solely the owners.

Up to this point I have been concerned solely with the measurement of the profit a corporation has earned. Economists rarely concern themselves with what has happened. Their interest, like that of businessmen, is in what will happen — the evaluation of alternative decisions about allocation of resources. In other words, How should and how do business firms make decisions about investments, production, prices, and related matters? I have not taken up these questions, and perhaps I should explain why. Recall that I agreed with Hicks that the solutions to investment, price, and other such problems of economic decision do not raise questions of measurement of profit. In selecting among alternative courses of action, the decision-maker asks, What are the future cash flows associated with each alternative? In a world of certainty, the future cash flows associated with each decision are known, and they may be summarized in a single figure of merit, such as rate of return.

When the future is uncertain, the problem becomes quite difficult. First, obtaining information about each alternative is an important and difficult task. Second, realistic and meaningful information about a decision will take the form of probability statements about the cash flows in each period. Third, the attractiveness of a decision will not depend only on its expected rate of return. At a minimum, the riskiness of the future cash flows will also influence the decision. Economists, operations researchers, and behavioral scientists, as well as accountants and people in other functional areas of business, are making progress on the formulation and use of decision models on a variety of fronts. However, as I stated earlier, progress in these areas has been impeded by problems of measurement of profit.

72

+ + +   CARL L. NELSON

An Accountant's View of Profit Measurement

THE measurement of profits is the peculiar province of the accountant; the process by which such profit measurement is to be performed
constitutes an important part of the subject matter of accounting. However, the accountant does not operate in a vacuum — he is influenced by
traditions going back at least five centuries, by important consumers
of accounting data such as bankers and investment analysts, by provisions of the Internal Revenue Code, by opinions of the staff and
commissioners of the Securities and Exchange Commission, and by
pressures of management that wishes to turn accounting to its own
ends. The accountant's ability to take independent actions is therefore
severely limited. His position is further weakened by the fact that, although most financial statements issued to the public are accompanied
by the accountant's opinion stating that they are "in conformity with
generally accepted principles," no one, not even the accountant, knows
exactly what an accounting principle is or what is meant by "generally
accepted."

   The accounting methodology used today is not far removed from that
used in the fifteenth century. The technical methods of processing the
data have been revolutionized; the internal reporting methods have
changed tremendously. For external reporting, however, accountants
are still using the same model that was used in the fifteenth century.
Refinements have been made, but the end product is surprisingly similar. The conceptual process used for the corporation with millions of
stockholders, a large investment in physical plant, and a life indefi-
nitely long is basically the same as that which was used for the one-man

enterprise or the small partnership with almost no investment in physical plant and a life in some cases of less than a year. The accounting model of the fifteenth century was not designed to be used in the dynamic economy of today, which is characterized by rapid changes in tastes and technology.

One problem is that we have not explicitly determined what we want to measure. Up until some time during the decade of the 1930's, the accountant prepared a "profit and loss" statement, which concluded with a figure described as "net profit." Terminology has changed, so that typically this report is now called an "income" statement and concludes with an item called "net income." It has been hypothesized that the causes of this change were the combined influence of income tax terminology (it is income that is taxed, not profits), the belief that "profits" is a term with undesirable, anti-social connotations, and the belief that "income" is a more inclusive term than "profit." As an alternative, current practice frequently uses the terms "earnings statement" and "earnings."

It is possible that all three of these terms (i.e., profits, income, earnings) refer to the same quantum, but the contrary may also be true. The concept of profit can be illustrated by the simple situation of a firm's manufacturing a product and selling it. The difference between the sales price and the cost of producing and selling that product is its profit. There are certain transactions that produce an inflow of cash (the sales); there are other transactions that produce an outflow of cash (the costs). The difference between the two flows is the profit. The cash inflow and cash outflow might not take place in the same period as the sale, but the cash flows are related to the sales of the period. Historically (at least in relatively recent history), this is the procedure that accountants have followed.

If it is profit in the sense of gain on transactions that the accountant is attempting to measure, the problem is probably unsolvable. Transactions may be discrete individually (that is, they occur one at a time) but to deal in totals is to remove the discreteness and to create a continuity. One of the most obvious problems is that related to plant and equipment costs, which are incurred in one period but are related to sales of later periods. It is conceivable that we could attack this problem and allocate these costs over the period of use in some kind of sensible way. By present standards, the cost is to be distributed "in a systematic and rational manner" (AICPA ARB 43); in practice, the distribution of cost may be systematic but it certainly is not rational. But how does one solve the problem of costs of research and development and of advertising? How can one associate these with individual units of product? These costs are ordinarily charged to the period in which they are incurred, but ordinarily none of the first two costs and not all of the last cost are related to sales for this period; hence, we know that current practice is faulty.

In many cases we do not know whether any favorable results will be secured; we do not know the period over which they will materialize; we certainly have even less idea about their distribution over this unknown period. It is possible, of course, that such expenditures are really expenditures of profit — bread cast upon the waters with no hope that it will be returned a thousandfold and only a faint hope of any return at all. Present accounting treatment might then be justified, but it is to be hoped that this is not the basis for these disbursements (although decreasing such expenditures in years of decreasing business activity on the grounds that "we can't afford it" might appear to present some evidence that this is what these expenditures are). This approach assumes that each year is independent — that what occurs in this period will have no effect on future years. Unfortunately, this assumption does not conform with the facts. The prices that a firm charges and the quantity it sells will affect demand in the future. Even costs of labor are not independent; with the existence of unemployment insurance and the growth of the guaranteed wage or supplementary unemployment benefits, the decision to employ or not to employ, to retain or not to retain, will affect cost of labor in the future.

On the other hand, it is possible that the accountant is really not attempting to measure profit in this sense but rather attempting to measure something quite different that may be called "income."

All conceivable approaches to measurement of income in this different sense can probably be described in terms of a definition of income formulated by the English economist J. R. Hicks, "A man's income [is] the maximum amount which he can consume during a week, and still expect to be as well off at the end of the week as he was at the beginning."[1] To translate this into the terms of a corporation, "consume" can be replaced by "the amount paid in dividends." The oper-

---

[1] *Value and Capital* (Oxford: Clarendon, 1939), p. 172.

ational questions then are: What is meant by "as well off"? and How does one measure how "well off" a business organization is? "Well-off-edness" is a purely psychological, subjective concept for which there is no absolute, no correct answer. It certainly is not correct to say that one is as well off as he thinks he is, but just as there are at least three approaches to determining the size of a room, there are several approaches to determining how well off a business unit is. It can be measured as money value (not as the term is used by accountants, but in terms of market value), as real value (a term easy to use, but impossible to define in any meaningful sense), as ownership of capacity to produce and sell, or even as position in the industry.

Historically, and continuing with minor deviations today, "well off" has been defined by the accountant in terms of money value. If one hypothesizes a corporation which starts with a cash investment of $1 million, pays dividends of $3 million over a thirty-year period, and then liquidates its assets and distributes $2 million to its stockholders, one can say that its income was $4 million over the thirty-year period.

To be forced to wait until the end of life of an enterprise (which might never come) will not satisfy the impatient consumer of accounting data. Knowing full well that in the long run we are all dead, more frequent measurements are demanded. The one-year period, probably reflecting our agricultural past and our worship of the sun, is well-nigh universal. One must therefore allocate portions of the $4 million to each of the thirty years.

In a sense the accountant does take this approach in that aggregate income over the life of the business is compatible with this concept, but in any one year there may be little relation between accounting income and changes in the money value of net assets. Changes in the value of intangible assets and unrealized changes in the value of tangible assets are not reflected in accounting income, and it is not likely that accountants — with their predilection for objectivity — will be inclined to extend their activities to these areas.

Quite obviously, if we cannot measure money income, we cannot measure real income. One of the additional difficulties is that we have not determined what is meant by "real income." It means income in terms of goods — an increase in purchasing power, but *what* purchasing power? Practicing and academic accountants interested in real income are apt to think of it as general purchasing power, but it is doubtful whether either management or stockholders are interested in general purchasing power. There is the implicit assumption in much of the literature in accounting, business finance, and economics that all prices vary together, and if this were true, there would be no problem. Unfortunately, this is not the real world. Management is interested in the ability to purchase buildings, equipment, labor, and material; stockholders are interested in their ability to purchase these items (to the extent of reinvestment either in this firm or in other firms) and to buy consumer's goods. Quite obviously, the goods that stockholders buy are not the goods purchased by those groups whose purchases are sampled for the Consumers' Price Index. Neither does the Implicit Price Deflator resulting from GNP calculations measure the price changes of interest to a particular corporation and its stockholders. It is time to turn away from a preoccupation with price averages and look at price behavior in general.

The position of a firm in an industry is subject to measurement in some sense, but the definition of the industry presents difficult problems. In addition, to call an improvement in position "income" is certainly using the word peculiarly, and to put this in dollars would appear to be impossible.

There remains the approach of measuring position by physical capacity. Evaluated by this concept, a firm is as well off if it has the same physical capacity to produce goods at the end of the period as it had at the beginning of the period. Technological advance then poses a problem. The question is whether a firm with a capacity of a hundred thousand units per year requiring a labor input of 200,000 hours is in a better position than it was when it had the same capacity but needed a labor input of 500,000 hours. By this approach, it is not in better position even though the new plant has a much higher cost than the old. The economic justification is that with rare exceptions the purchase of this new plant would be financed from internally generated funds, and hence these funds are not available for dividends. If the primary interest of the stockholder is in income which might be available for dividends, income is the amount left after deducting this necessary increase in investment. Some may agree with this point and extend the reasoning to include a deduction for the cost of expansion necessary to meet demand as the number of customers and the size of their incomes grow.

Profits in the Modern Economy

Regardless of what the accountant is trying to do, we can draw certain conclusions about how he does it. Reflecting the bias of bankers and short-term creditors and perhaps a necessity to offset the natural ebullience of dynamic management, the accountant's approach is conservative. Accountants do not recognize increases in the value of assets until they are realized — which means not until the assets are converted into cash or, more frequently, into a valid legal claim on a customer. Inventories, securities, and plant and equipment may increase in monetary value, but all these improvements in economic position (valued in dollars) are typically ignored by the accountant.

This same bias is reflected in the treatment of expenditures for assets and services. There is the tendency to charge as much of these as possible to current operations and to charge off those capitalized as rapidly as possible. Thus, expenditures for research and development, advertising, and employee development are considered to be charges against current revenues even though much, if not all, the benefit from these will be received in future years, just as is true of an expenditure for plant and equipment. In classifying expenditures on buildings and equipment as repairs (charged to current operations) or improvements (set up as an asset), the accountant is biased toward repairs. To use more specific illustrations: the magazine publisher may charge subscription costs to current operations even though past experience indicates the future will be benefited; the petroleum producer may charge so-called "intangible" drilling costs to current operations even though future oil flows will result; and the life insurance company charges the first-year agent's commission as a current cost even though this cost is disproportionately large and would not be incurred if the policy had a year's life.

Once costs are capitalized, the accountant usually is disposed to charge them to operations as rapidly as possible. Merchandise is written down if either replacement cost or selling price drops. The asset "plant and equipment" is usually amortized over a period that represents a pessimistic forecast rather than the expected value. There is pressure to amortize intangible assets arising from purchase over a short period of time. In the expectation of rising prices, LIFO is used as an inventory method. Consolidated statements are issued that do not include the operations of profitable non-dividend-paying subsidiaries.

It may be that Henry Simons's categorization of an accountant is correct, namely: "The reputable accountant never loses sight of the fact that his income statements are influential in matters of dividend policy. Income, for him, is perhaps only what may be reported safely to unsophisticated directors as income. He aims, it would seem, never to ascertain what income is in any really definable sense, but rather to devise rules of calculation which will make the result a minimum or at least give large answers only in the future. Conventional accounting, moreover, not only employs a procedure with a markedly conservative bias, but, promptly repudiates this procedure whenever it shows signs of working the other way."[2]

One approach to determining what the accountant does is to say that he does not measure income in any absolute sense, but rather in a relative sense. The argument goes thus: To say the income of United States Steel for 1963 is $203 million is to say nothing in an absolute sense, but to say that the income increased from $164 million to $203 million is to give meaningful information. Although this may be correct in general, the meaningfulness of the change is of low order of magnitude unless the absolute amounts are meaningful. Furthermore, under present permissible accounting methods, an increase in reported income may not necessarily reflect anything that would be called an improvement in any non-accounting sense.

Primary attention is being given today to narrowing differences in accounting treatment of various revenues and expenses. Such items as stock options, pension costs, long-term leases, deferred income taxes, intangible developmental costs for oil companies, intercorporate investments, and investment credits can be and are being treated differently by different firms. In the opinion of many accountants, this leads to confusion, lack of comparability, and consequent failure of seekers of information to use accounting data; their remedy would be to lay down principles that would result in using the same methods of accounting under substantially similar conditions.

Such an aim is commendable, but it would appear that some accountants would carry this to the extreme of endorsing uniformity regardless of the agreed methods of uniformity. In other words, uniformity is to be achieved whether the resulting data have any significance or meaning at all. The goal should, rather, be to determine what kind of accounting data would assist the consumer to make better economic decisions and then to produce these data.

[2] *Personal Income Taxation* (Chicago: University of Chicago Press, 1938), p. 81.

Profits in the Modern Economy

One approach the accountant might take is to develop a concept of income which is economically significant and yet operational. It is possible that an income oriented toward capacity would meet these specifications.

A second approach would be to measure something that the accountant calls "income" (or profits) and that consumers of accounting data can rely upon because they know that there is uniform practice among all accountants and because they have faith in the competence of accountants. It may have no economic significance, but the decision-maker will never know this; he will never know that he has been led astray because he will blame the unpredictable events of the modern dynamic world rather than his accounting data for his mistakes. Accounting data then become a more expensive Miltown — a non-oral tranquilizer.

A third possibility is to abandon the idea of presenting a measurement of income and to substitute various kinds of information in an annual report. Included in this report might be: (1) measure of activity during the year — volume of sales classified by product and by area and volume of production classified by product and by area and measured by sales price, material cost, and labor cost; (2) year-end cost functions by product; (3) production capacity for various products (but capacity itself is a tricky concept); (4) cost of current capacity; (5) reproduction cost of current capacity; (6) engineering estimates of probable remaining life of capacity; (7) cash-flow statement; (8) amount of research expenditures (can "research" be defined?); (9) amount of advertising expenditures; and (10) a description of manpower development programs.

Perhaps the most useful information would be publication of the plans of management concerning the quantity and price of goods sold, quantity and cost (not including amortization of outlays of previous years) of goods manufactured, outlays on selling costs, research, and so forth, at the beginning of the year, followed by a report of actual events with an explanation of significant variances. The danger of this, of course, is that the plans would undoubtedly be affected by the reluctance of management to display them before the public. This reluctance is understandable. Anything new is always terrifying to a human being, and fear of competitors is sometimes an imagined, sometimes a real threat. The pure profit of the economist exists because of imperfections of the market. Information removes imperfections, and hence removes what management wishes to maximize.

To summarize, accounting information on profits represents the results of an imperfect measuring system manned by imperfect human beings. Valuable as the information may be, it is subject to misuse, and among the individuals most likely to misuse it are imperfectly informed scholars and practitioners in economics and finance.

Profits from the Investor's Point of View

THE story is told of a bird who went to work every day. He gave his wife an affectionate peck as he picked up his briefcase and lunch and set out for work, from which he came back every evening. He was, however, a bit careless; he did not always fly over the public highway, but instead took shortcuts over private property. One summer day, he came home terribly battered and bruised, his briefcase lost, his feathers awry. His wife, after attending to his immediate needs, asked, "Whatever in the world happened?" "Well," he replied, "I was taking a shortcut over a lawn and I noticed that the people had put down there some white lines on the grass and they were running around playing a game. So I went down to see what the game was all about, and I suddenly discovered I was in the game myself." It seems to me that what happened to this bird who fell into a game of badminton is what has happened to the idea of profits.

"Profits" in this conference have been batted, twisted, referred to as tranquilizers, and even said to be taxed completely out of existence — and still there are profits for us to discuss. It is important to remember, for all this debate about what profits are, that they still do come through and get home as the bird did. Although the bird learned his lesson and stayed away from that particular game, it is unfortunate that profits have to run a gauntlet every fiscal year. Business managers have to decide how to make them, although the accountants and the economists say that one can never be quite sure what they are, or how much profits have been made.

In this paper I want to turn away from such questions as the determination of profits, either in the form of earnings as reported by the accountant or as measures necessary within the firm, to the question of what profits mean to the owners of the business. After all, if the firm is to make investments, it is able to do so only because others have made investments in it, and I want to explore the needs of the investor in terms of profit. This requires us to consider the motives of the individual which can be classed as economic. I once said that if I ever met a purely economic man, I could not tolerate him because he would certainly be the most grasping and disagreeable person I ever saw — but I have never met him. Of course, the so-called "economic man" is only a portion of the whole man; but it is his economic judgment that dominates his choice of whether to place resources in investments or in more immediate pleasures.

Despite many statements to the contrary, I suggest that earnings are not what the investor wants. In his essay Professor Carl L. Nelson observed that the shareholder is interested in dividends; that if there are no dividends then there is no income for the investor. Agreeing with this, I say that an investor will commit his liquid funds to a security only if, in his judgment, it is more desirable than other securities available to him with comparable conditions of amount, time, and certainty of flows of funds from the firm to the investor. The flow of funds from the firm to the investor is a dimension I wish to discuss, for it is the source of value that attracts the economic side of a man's judgment.

It is not enough to have the firm reporting to the investor that it has produced internally enough cash flows to maintain productive capacity. The firm must also be able to promise, in one form or another, a value to the investor which will induce him (and those who follow as further funds are needed) to make additional investments in the firm and not to turn elsewhere. The obligation of management to the investor is to plan the inflows and outflows of the firm (including the payment of dividends, the acceptance of expansion projects, and the arrangement of the terms of security contracts) with the goal of maximizing the value of the equity interest in the firm as that interest existed at the moment of the management's choice. At this point, I am obviously disagreeing with Myron J. Gordon's idea that management now has obligations to all kinds of interests. Although it is true that society is making some of these other obligations more burdensome upon management (as is certainly the privilege of a democratic society), it is clear from the arithmetic of profit making that there must be one interest left over — the residual one — that has the privilege of participating in any excess of values the firm may produce. This, I believe, is a dimension of profits that has not yet been suggested here. Profit is the gain in value that takes place in a period. It may be consumed to show it is a gain, but it is nevertheless a gain; the question is, To whom does it accrue? In my opinion, in a private corporation it accrues to the owners of the equity interest.

Starting with this proposition, I turn to what the stockholder observes in determining how the value of his investment is faring. Instead of assuming that earnings are the sole object of a stockholder's attention when he evaluates his investment, let us examine the matter more closely. It appears almost immediately that the amount of earnings can be only a representative of other things, and not a very accurate one at that, if we are to listen to Professor Nelson and others, who are surely right. The amount of earnings can be only a representative of other things because, so far as an investor can be regarded as an economic man, his estimate of the value of an investment will result only from his estimate of the flow of funds he will receive after taxes. The investor can assign no value to any act of the firm whose securities he holds unless that act changes his expectations about his future flows of funds, about their timing, and/or about the degree of certainty of these expectations. The mere fact that earnings are to be retained has no value to the shareholder. The operative questions are: What will the shareholder receive? When will he receive it? How sure is it? Only under fully idealized neoclassical conditions (to use Professor John Lintner's words [1]) could the amount of earnings become an accurate representation of such receipts.

Most of those who have investigated this area with any care will find little reason to quarrel with the proposition that the value of an investment to its owner can be described as made up of several factors; each factor is emphasized by each investor according to the need he expects this particular investment to fulfill as a part of his investment portfolio. For analytical purposes, I suggest that the model of the economic value of an investment to its owner be expressed as the sum of

[1] "Dividends, Earnings, Leverage, Stock Prices and the Supply of Capital to Corporations," *Review of Economics and Statistics*, XLIV (August 1962), 247.

the present value of three groups of expectations measured over a time period that the investor considers suitable for holding the security in question.

The first element of value from the shareholder's point of view is derived from the existing cash distribution (it might be zero), considered as continuing and capitalized at a rate reflecting the return suitable to the degree of certainty of this assumed distribution. This element of value will be considered after taxes, and it will enter into the individual's consideration in proportion to the importance of steady income to him. This element of value I term the *level income factor.*

The second element of value is derived from an anticipated change in the dividend (it may be up or down) as it occurs at various times, capitalized at a rate reflecting the degree of certainty of growth or shrinkage, considered after taxes, and entering the total value according to the importance of change in income to the stockholder. This is the *changing income factor.* It has recently received considerable attention in the literature and practice of investment analysis; in fact, the idea that the value of a stock depends not only on the current income but also on the growth is almost unanimously accepted at the present time.

The third element of value is derived from the anticipated capital gain or loss at the time of the liquidation of the investment. It, too, will be capitalized after taxes at a rate reflecting the certainty of the event, and it will be added to the value according to the importance of its expectation to the shareholder. This is the *capital gain factor.*

In my view, we cannot condense this tripartite formulation without assuming idealized conditions of certainty, information, and so forth that do not exist. Careful studies of investors will show that they use different rates of capitalization in the three factors; certainly they anticipate different levels of expectation, and many of them prefer cash returns to equal increases in price during the period that they hold stock. In short, one must assume a fully idealized economic man, as well as other ideal conditions, before the proposed formulation can be compressed into any briefer form, although a briefer form is simpler to calculate and is used in most of the economic literature.

To say that the investor establishes the value of his investments from a level of income, anticipated changes in that level, and ultimate capital gain or loss is to describe areas of emphasis that can be accepted easily by the persons who have been working in the field of investment analysis or stockholder relations. Review the results of surveys of stockholders, talk to investment counselors, meet retired persons who refuse to consume anything but funds received as dividends, consult wealthy persons who are worried about taxation and would prefer almost anything to a cash dividend, think of your own reasons for investing, and you will agree not only that this tripartite formulation is a recognizable abstraction from actual practice but also that a different basis of evaluation is often applied to each of the three types of funds flows I have identified. If this seems irrational, look to your assumptions, which I suggest you will find have taken you far from the real world.

It follows that the process of deciding upon dividend policies is the process of management that determines the value the shareholder finds in the investment he holds. It is a formidable task to make decisions in this area; and research using advanced techniques is needed. I want to suggest a few things about the kind of thinking and study that needs to be undertaken.

First, each management is concerned not with stockholders in general, but with the stockholders of its own firm at the moment that the decision is being made. Two brief examples show the possible difference. Electric utility firms know there is persuasive evidence that shareholders who buy utility stocks are immensely interested in current dividends and in the prospect for their immediate growth. Clearly, the management of such firms should be thinking about large payouts. By contrast, the management of a firm entirely owned by one individual, who has the fortune (or misfortune) to be paying 97 per cent of his income in taxes, has little concern about current dividends; its problem is to find ways of investing internally generated funds within the firm — ways which will produce any rate of return higher than 3 per cent. And so it goes, from firm to firm.

Thus the question arises, How does management learn the needs of its investors? Except for the relatively few (but very important) firms that are "open corporations" (a term I substitute for the confusing words "public company"), a particular firm has a particular group of identifiable owners. In any such closed corporation, the management can be expected to know in detail the owning groups and how these groups evaluate their interests in the firm. The groups may have fully rational interests, but not wholly economic ones. Getting this knowledge is difficult; yet it is usually made easier by the relative smallness of the group and by the low turnover in ownership. It is hoped that there will not be major conflicts of interest among the owners.

In open corporations, the stockholders can be considered as investors willing to be buyers or sellers of parts of their holdings according to their estimates of relative advantage. The dissatisfied may liquidate his interest at will. The management of such a firm, I suggest, may fulfill its responsibility by carrying out policies that produce the highest market value. In this respect, some recent work by Daniel M. Holland and Paul H. Cootner is stimulating, because they have realized that many evaluations investors are making are decisions to trade off. One cannot ask the shareholder such a simple question as, Would you like more dividends? but, rather, one must ask him, Would you like to have an increase in dividends of $X instead of a rise in price of $Y?

Hence, a private corporation cannot attract funds simply by attending to reported earnings per share, because earnings per share are printed on a kind of paper that is not negotiable. The investor must be offered something which he can touch or expect to touch in the form of money; present dividends, anticipated dividends, or hopes for capital gain — if he is to be persuaded to invest in a particular security. Otherwise, he will turn elsewhere.

Another thing, often neglected, that is necessary for establishing the conditions of profitability from the investor's point of view is the case of expansion through the sale of new shares to other than the present shareholders. Clearly, new shares must be sold by many expanding companies from time to time, but this course has been accepted much too readily by many managements as the solution to a problem for which alternative solutions should be considered.

I take as given that the primary concern of management is with the interest of the group of owners who, at the time the expansion is being considered and before it takes place, hold all the equity. If new shares are issued, the present group will hold only a portion of the equity in the future. Under such circumstances, actions that promise to increase the value of the entire equity may sometimes reduce the value of the portion of it remaining in the hands of the previous owners. This consequence should be avoided by management wherever possible. I refer, of course, to dilution.

Profits in the Modern Economy

Dilution has been defined almost universally by investment analysts as an increase in the number of shares without a corresponding increase in assets and earning power. The criterion implicit in this definition begs an important question because it combines one factor, which tends to lower value — namely, the issue of new shares — with other factors — such as increased earnings — that tend to increase value. We must adopt a measure which focuses attention separately on the negative aspect, the increase in the number of shares. Once we know the size of this negative force in a particular case, we shall be ready to search for positive factors to justify the financing. In order to clarify the vocabulary widely in use, I propose that dilution in the sense defined above be termed "net dilution," since this is the effect of the two forces, whatever they may be. The value of the reducing factor in this net dilution may be termed "immediate dilution" and defined as: "relative loss or weakening of the equity position caused by the issuing of new shares." Note that the reference is to the equity position of a certain group but not to the value of the equity as a total.

Suppose that we have a corporation with three shares outstanding, each of which is owned by a different shareholder. More money is needed for corporate purposes and can be raised by selling an outsider one new share. If this is done, then there are four shares and those who once held all the equity now hold three quarters of it. Under what circumstances might the three original shareholders approve such a change in the sharing of the interest of the business?

Those of the earnings-per-share school would say that if the total profits were increased by one third, then each of the original shareholders is where he was before. The total having been increased in this way, one can divide it by four and find the same earnings per share as before. This is true of earnings per share, and may be true of the immediate dividends. But if the original holders had been able to raise the needed money by borrowing instead of issuing a new share in equity, they could have participated in all future earnings instead of only three quarters of them. It is always better to keep the position of the equity intact and to turn to any form of financing other than new shares so long as such opportunities are possible, given the other policies and constraints of the corporation.

Further, I propose that those concerned with financing must attend not only to the immediate effect of the financing upon earnings per share but also to the restoration of the rate of growth, so that the expectations of the original shareholders are not damaged in that dimension either. All this leads me to the following test for such a situation: the value of the investment of an equity group facing dilution will not be restored unless the ratio of the value of the new investment to the value of the existing equity at least equals the ratio of the number of new shares to the number of original shares. So, for example, in the case above, if the number of shares is increased by one third, the management must attend to corporate practices so that the value of the total equity interest will increase by one third. That value, I repeat, does not lie solely in immediate earnings per share or in dividends but also in expectations of growth.

Most of the preceding papers have been concerned about the measurement of profits as an internal matter, and in that respect Professor Gordon's comments about turning from accounting profits to other measures for achieving a measurement of adequacy of management are closest to my opinion. But profits also attract funds to the individual firm and, speaking broadly, attract the savings of society to the entire free enterprise system, a system we all value highly. Looking upon profits as earnings per share is not enough. Management must see the obligation and need to attend to the source of value for the investor. This obligation is met only when profits get through to him, now or in the future, in monetary form.

Comments   HOWARD G. SCHALLER

I SHALL consider Carl Nelson's paper first, then Myron Gordon's and, briefly, Pearson Hunt's. It appears to me that Nelson has concluded that the present state of income measurement is very unsatisfactory in that: (1) there is no consensus on what should be measured; and (2) many of the activities of modern firms could not be satisfactorily handled even if there were a consensus on the first point. He gives as examples of the second, research and development and advertising expenditures. In reply, I would say that nobody expects the accountant to measure the unmeasurable and that the accountant's methods will always be subject to debate. The solution to Nelson's dilemma appears to be his own suggestion that a concept of income that is economically significant and yet operational be developed. If such a concept were developed, and the accountant then disclosed the methods he used to measure the income and presented the data necessary to calculate income by other methods, the consumer of the accounting data would be well served. At least, this is the best that can be done under the circumstances. Nelson suggests two other solutions: the first, to regard accounting data as a non-oral tranquilizer (he advances this facetiously, I take it, and thus would be willing to abandon it), and the second, to abandon the measure of income and substitute a variety of other types of information in its place. I would not accept abandonment of income measurement, on the grounds that some over-all measurement of the performance of management is needed; here I agree with Gordon. Giving data on income and the other activities as Nelson suggests would actually represent a dichotomy. It appears to me that a company should provide much of this information so the shareholder can make a sound judgment about his investment. The statement of current income alone would not be enough to support a sound judgment since, as Hunt points out, the shareholder will want to anticipate future dividend rates and asset prices.

As I see it, Gordon is considering three different methods of measuring income: (1) the historical cost method, (2) the Hicksian method, and (3) the replacement cost method. Gordon rejects the first two and retains the third, and I agree with him. The historical cost method is inadequate because the estimate of current income, or income during the current period, is influenced by price changes that occurred between an older period and the current period. Gordon seems to reject the Hicksian method on the grounds of certain technical difficulties with the concept plus the fact that the concept was designed for a purpose other than calculating the profits of a business enterprise. I am not so sure that the Hicksian method is wanting on the grounds of technical difficulties specified by Gordon — that the method assumes certainty and infinite life. Although I am not prepared to develop this point, it does appear that the Hicksian method might be rescued by attaching probability distributions to various possible outcomes and thus creating the basis for estimating expected future receipts. The major difficulty is, as Gordon suggests, that the Hicksian method does not provide an adequate basis for evaluating the performance of management during a given period. Hicks developed his definition to shed light on the decisions about consumption by individuals, not to measure the income of business firms. Gordon has made this point, and it has also been developed at some length by Maurice Moonitz.[1]

Although the Hicksian concept may prove useful to the individual investor, it does not necessarily yield a measure satisfactory for evaluating the performance of management during the current period. According to Gordon, the Hicksian method may tell the farmer something about the wisdom of his decision in becoming a farmer, but not tell him much about how well he did during the current year, given the fact that he was a farmer.

Thus, the difficulty with the Hicksian method is that it does not tell how well management is managing the resources available during the current period. The evaluation of the performance of management is essential to both the manager and the owner. If the consequences of past decisions are bad, presumably the manager would want to know this so that he can alter his decision-making, and the owner would want to know this, among other facts, for evaluating his investment. It seems that the evaluation of the performance of management is the essential issue in the measurement of profits. But, accepting this as a goal of measuring profits and considering the replacement cost method as being the best way to attain the goal, I raise two further questions:

First, will measurement of profit really provide information needed by the decision maker for future decisions? As Edgar O. Edwards and Philip W. Bell have pointed out in their *The Theory and Measurement of Business Income*,[2] the principal function of accounting data is to evaluate the outcome of the course of action chosen from among all those available. The accounting data do not tell us whether the chosen one was, in fact, the optimum one. Moreover, even if the results of the past decisions turn out to be good in the absolute, what guideline is this for the future when optimization has not been considered? Gordon seems to say that as long as profits are good management will have little incentive to change — it will be cautious and make changes only on a small scale. If this is so, management certainly needs some additional, and powerful, evaluative tools. The question, then, is whether

[1] "Should We Discard the Income Concept?" *Accounting Review*, XXXVII, No. 2 (April 1962), 175–180.
[2] (Berkeley and Los Angeles: University of California Press, 1961), pp. 3–6.

accounting systems designed for replacement cost calculation can generate the data needed for the development of these tools.

Second, will the profit calculations that have been endorsed provide a proper means for directing allocations of resources? Gordon seems to raise this question himself when he states that the Hicksian method may evaluate the decision to become a farmer but not the actual performance once the decision has been made.

If the replacement cost method does not evaluate both, is there a satisfactory measure? I suspect that Gordon's definition of profits — i.e., sales, net of current cost, and the labor and assets used to attain the revenue — would yield data that would permit, at least in a crude way, the necessary comparison. This is certainly a point that needs to be clarified.

Comments   JOEL E. SEGALL

I SHOULD like to describe these three papers as stimulating and provocative — except that in George Stigler's lexicon if you describe someone else's paper as "stimulating," what you mean is that the author has made a mistake. If you describe it as "provocative," you mean he is absolutely wrong, he said nothing right.

I do not mean that. The titles for these papers were well chosen. There are only *views* of profit measurement, and these views are neither right nor wrong; they are only more or less relevant.

The three papers have much in common. Each asserts that when we talk about "profit measurement" we don't know exactly *what* we should measure; that *whatever* it is that accountants do wind up measuring, they measure very badly indeed; that what we measure must depend on *why* we measure it — that is, for whose use we are making the measurement. Similarly, all three papers invoke J. R. Hicks, which is always wise. Gordon, however, would bury Hicks, although he is somehow essentially in agreement with the Hicksian concept; Hunt would dig Hicks up again; Nelson would use Hicks's skeleton as a framework for evaluating different ways of measuring profits.

There is another thing these papers have in common and that is this: I had trouble understanding them. Three authorities were asked to explain how to measure a variable in which all three have a profound professional interest. One (Gordon) tells us to use current cost. One (Hunt) tells us to use a cash return expectation method. One (Nelson) throws up his hands and tells us to abandon all hope.

Now these answers are just about as far apart as it's possible to be, and I think that's impressive — especially considering the fact that not one of the three recommendations is for the method of measuring profits currently in use. Therefore, I presume that each author would dispute each of the other two and that all three would dispute the rest of the world. In view of this, I should be forgiven my difficulties in understanding the papers.

Let me consider some of the points with which I have problems. The Hicks-Alexander solution is to measure profits, or income, during a given period of time as cash receipts plus, or minus, the change in the present value of expected future cash receipts. One can take the position of the stockholder and think of the market value of the stock as being something like the present value of expected receipts. That solution is described as a cash-flow concept of profits in a paper by Diran Bodenhorn.[1] To measure stockholders' profits by the cash-flow concept, one adds up the cash dividends paid during the year, plus any price appreciation in his stock or minus any price decline. The profits may be expressed as a rate of return by finding the rate of discount that equates the present value of the dividends plus the price at the end of the year to the initial price of the stock.

I shall relate this concept to the Gordon paper. Gordon observed that the Hicks concept is designed to help make decisions about consumption. But, for that restricted use, he finds the concept faulty. He demonstrates this by describing an individual whose net cash receipts, including now the change in the market value of the stock, result in a loss of $9,500 during the period. Gordon asks how the individual is aided in deciding on consumption by learning that his loss is $9,500. He points out that an individual who "believes firmly that he should only spend his income would have an extremely difficult time." Now this may be true. The individual may, indeed, have an extremely difficult time, but the difficult time arises from his firmly held belief and not from the way his income is measured. Apparently he has sustained a loss. Of course, he has a difficult time, and if he is silly enough to

[1] Reproduced below, pp. 98–116.

believe that he should spend only his income, he will have an even more difficult time. But the method of measurement should not be blamed. This may be an incorrect interpretation of Gordon. What probably underlies Gordon's example is the notion that, since the individual already knows the market value of his stock at the beginning and the end of each period and his cash receipts during the period, clearly the computation of the loss is redundant. This is true; the stockholder already has that information. But I fail to see how that fact can be a repudiation of the concept. It just seems unreasonable — or I do not understand the point — that present values and cash flow are relevant to making decisions about consumption but that somehow the sum of these is not. I do not doubt that Gordon will concur that I did not quite understand his paper, but let me go on.

For purposes of evaluating managerial performance, Gordon chooses the current cost concept and in doing so rejects, among other things, that lovable concept, present value. This he does because "including capital gains or losses, realized or unrealized, in the income figure, distorts its meaning." Now the idea is clear — changes in the value of the firm are beyond the control of the manager and, therefore, are not relevant in evaluating managerial performance. But that is not necessarily true. Even the farmer of Gordon's example frequently has the option of using his land in a more or less exhausting fashion. He might produce more of a given crop now and perhaps reduce future crop yields. Such a choice can conceivably reduce the present value of the land — its market value. This action is clearly the result of a managerial decision, and the farm manager should be evaluated in the light of such decision.

As for business firms, it is easy to think of circumstances in which managers enter into contracts that have violent impacts on the value of the firm, or the value of the common stock, plus an impact on reported earnings. Consider the current diversification fad. Assume that a manager initiates a diversification program to stabilize income or, perhaps, cash flows. That is, he acquires another firm whose fortunes are exactly the opposite of those of the current firm, and so reduces risk per dollar of investment. The average income may remain unchanged, but the value of the firm has changed; I suggest that this was a wise move by management, and management should be rewarded for it. Or consider the purchase for inventory of a commodity with a highly volatile price.

I find it difficult to believe that managers are indifferent to the prices at which they acquire the commodity. I must confess that Gordon's department store is a shaking example, although I suspect that department stores generally are examples of business firms whose commodities do not fluctuate very greatly in price.

Let me reverse this example a little. I must believe that if Marshall Field can buy for inventory a commodity whose price is expected to rise in the future, it will bunch up its purchases and buy now rather than later. This is wise. It is a managerial decision that results in a capital gain and I think we have to account for it. In fact, I should expect these things to be generally true. Actions such as recognizing that there are price movements in commodities seem clearly within the province of responsible management and are not only appropriately but desirably so.

I should, for example, consider the management of a steel-using firm singularly remiss if it leaves out of its consideration the likelihood of a steel strike and the consequent shortage and rise in price of steel. A management which correctly foresees this should be rewarded, and one which does not foresee it penalized. I believe such rewards and penalties are precluded if one follows Gordon's advice and excludes capital gains and losses from profits.

Having stated all this, I do recognize that there are probably classes of events that are beyond the control and even beyond any forecasting ability of management. It would be nice if it were possible to correct for these events. I don't know how. In short, Gordon's method does not provide enough information to evaluate management, and the Hicks-Alexander solution — or the variant of it that has been proposed — provides too much information.

It is at this point that Nelson's primrose path begins to look like the highway of virtue. "Forget it," says Nelson; "the current state of knowledge does not permit us to resolve these difficulties. Don't try to report profits, instead give information about those elements that affect profits and evaluate managerial performance on the basis of specific decisions in specific areas." This, I believe, is wise. If the management decides to market a new product, an intelligent evaluation requires knowing something about what is happening with that new product and that something is not necessarily incorporated in conventional earnings figures. In short, I agree with Nelson, but to stop here and admit failure takes the joy out of life. Speculation and dispute, it seems to me, provide the fun and games of academic life, and we are not at all afraid of Virginia Woolf.

Hunt has explicitly confined himself to examining profits from the viewpoint of the investor as distinct from measuring profit for managerial appraisal. This is clever — perhaps ingenious is a better word — but I don't think we should let him get away with it. Hunt observes that the proper job of management is to maximize the value of stockholders' interest. But if he is telling how to measure the stockholders' interest (and he is), then he is inevitably telling something about the measurement of profits for evaluation of managers. What he tells us is that profits should be measured by net cash flows to stockholders, including changes in prices of stock.

I am puzzled, though, by his analysis of stockholder dilution. Hunt says that management should seek desperately for ways of financing other than new stock flotation, but he includes retention of earnings among the other ways of financing. His idea is that stock flotation impairs the anticipated growth of earnings and, presumably, dividends and so reduces the value of the stockholders' interests. But since stock flotation is a substitute for earnings retention, the consequent variation in dividends must not be ignored. That is, if earnings are retained to finance a project, then less will be paid currently in dividends; current stockholders will have increased their investment in the firm and will be the sole recipients of future dividends. If the alternative, stock flotation, is chosen, then more will be paid currently as dividends since the firm should not be presumed to hold idle capital; current stockholders will have a smaller investment in the firm, and will no longer be the sole recipients of future dividends. I contend that, except for tax liabilities, the two alternatives have exactly the same impact on stockholders. In the one case, stockholders get more now and less later (stock flotation) and in the other they get less now and more later (earnings retention). I should like to see Hunt elaborate his model and treat this case explicitly.

I should like to go on record at least once as asserting what I believe will be the most fruitful approach to measurement of profit. Probably the most important class of decisions managers must make is that of capital budgeting. The generally recommended method for dealing with capital investment problems is to estimate the net cash flows gen-

96

erated by an investment project, discount these cash flows by the cost of capital, and get the present value. If the present value is positive, presumably the project would be profitable and should be undertaken.

The present value so derived, it seems to me, is nothing more than the increment in the value of stockholders' interest, and the best measurement of that is the change in the value of the common stock. In short, just as the profitability of a project is evaluated by the cash flows to the firm, discounted by the cost of capital, so should managerial performance and profitability be evaluated by net cash flows to stockholders, including changes in the value of stock. The changes in the value of the stock must, of course, be taken in relation to the market as a whole. Frankly, I do not have time to explain just *how* this should be done.

+ + +   DIRAN BODENHORN

A Cash-Flow Concept of Profit

THE traditional theory of the firm is based on the assumption that the firm acts in the stockholders' interests, that the stockholders are interested in profit, and, therefore, that the objective of the firm is to maximize profit. There have been many theoretical discussions of the concept of profit, but there is no consensus on the precise definition of this theoretical construct.[1] Nevertheless, the theory of the firm has been based on the assumption of profit maximization, and profit has been thought of (loosely) as the difference between the revenue received from the product sold and the payments made to the productive factors that together produced that product.

This concept of profit has been difficult to apply to investment decisions, and concepts about maximization of wealth and about cash flow have been developed in connection with the problem. This paper presents a cash-flow concept of profit which is associated with the cash-flow theory of stock value. This concept of profit has three desirable properties which make it more useful than the traditional concept: (1) It can be used in decision-making within the firm since maximization of profit is in the stockholders' interest. (2) The profit of the firm coincides with the stockholders' income in each time period. (3)

NOTE: Reprinted, with permission, from the *Journal of Finance*, XIX (March 1964), 16–31.

The author is indebted to many friends for innumerable discussions of the concept of profit over many years. Professors Alan Batchelder and Robert Gallman have been particularly helpful in discussing the organization and content of this paper.
[1] See, for example, J. Fred Weston, "The Profit Concept and Theory: A Restatement," *Journal of Political Economy*, LXII (April 1954), 152–170.

Past profit can be measured from market values so that it is an objective measure of performance.

Net cash flows are defined in the second section of this paper as the cash flows between the firm and its stockholders. The value of the stock is then the present value of the future net cash flows. In the third section cash-flow profit is defined as the increase in the stock value plus the net cash flow of the period. If the expectations for the period are fulfilled and those for the future are unchanged, a normal profit is made on the initial stock value (investment). If expectations change, pure profits arise.

The cash-flow concept is then compared to the traditional concept. The fourth section discusses the handling of depreciation, a concept not required in cash-flow analysis. It is shown that depreciation expenses understate capital costs unless implicit interest is charged on the book value of net worth. It follows in the fifth section that the traditional profit concept cannot be used in decision-making unless this implicit interest is charged as an expense. It develops, however, that the decision is independent of the pattern of depreciation, which confirms the cash-flow analysis.

In the sixth section it is shown that cash-flow profit coincides with stockholders' income in every time period, since it is based on the return which the stockholder would get if the firm liquidated as a going concern. Traditional profit is based on the return the stockholders would get if the firm liquidated its assets piecemeal instead of as a going concern, and it is therefore of less economic interest. The last section points out briefly the advantages of having a concept of profit which can be measured from market values.

CASH FLOWS AND STOCK VALUATION

In this section I present a definition of cash flows and a theory of stock pricing based on cash-flow analysis.[2] A careful definition of cash

[2] For further discussion and justification of cash-flow analysis, see Diran Bodenhorn, "Depreciation, Price Level Changes, and Investment Decisions," *Journal of Business*, XXXVI (October 1963), 448–457, and also "On the Problem of Capital Budgeting," *Journal of Finance*, LXVII (December 1959), 473–492; Joel Dean, "Measuring the Productivity of Capital," *Harvard Business Review*, XXXII, No. 1 (January–February 1954), 120–130 (reprinted in Ezra Solomon, *The Management of Corporate Capital* (Glencoe, Ill.: Free Press, 1959); and J. Lorie and L. J. Savage, "Three Problems in Capital Rationing," *Journal of Business*, XXVIII (October 1955), 229–239 (also reprinted in Solomon).

flows is required because previous discussions have been concerned with investment decisions rather than with stock pricing. They have therefore been concerned with the cash flows associated with a particular investment project, rather than with the flows to the firm as a whole, and we must recognize the possibility that cash flows generated by one project will be used to finance another project. Furthermore, other discussions tend to separate the investment decision from that about financing, and I want to include considerations of financing.

In defining cash flows, one needs to consider transactions involving goods or services, financial obligations, and cash balances. The purchase of any good or service, whether for current use (expense) or future use (asset), results in an immediate cash payment, by my definition. If in fact the goods are purchased on account, then a second transaction — the borrowing of money from the seller — is recorded. The sale of goods or services also results in an immediate cash receipt. If credit is extended, then a second transaction — the lending of money to the buyer — is also recorded.

With respect to financial transactions, I distinguish between transactions involving the financial obligations of the firm itself, i.e., obligations calling for a payment by the firm to someone outside the firm, and transactions involving the financial obligations of outsiders. Cash receipts and cash payments are defined to include all transactions with the financial obligations of outsiders.

In considering the firm's own obligations, it is useful to distinguish between debt and equity obligations. This distinction would not be important in a world of certainty. If everyone knew precisely what payments would be made on all financial obligations, all future payments would be discounted by the lender at the same interest rate, and the terms of the contract between the borrower and the lender would be irrelevant. In a world of uncertainty, however, the discount rate applied to equity obligations is higher than that applied to debt. This problem can be handled more readily if cash receipts and payments are defined to include transactions involving debt but to exclude those involving equity.

The problem of cash balances is somewhat peculiar. In a world of certainty it would be unprofitable for a firm to hold cash. Any cash not needed immediately to make payments would be lent at interest, since liquidity is worthless if all future cash needs can be perfectly foreseen, and there are no costs of flotation associated with lending, borrowing, or repaying money. But in a world of uncertainty, cash balances are held because they provide liquidity. In principle, the decision to purchase liquidity by increasing cash balances or to sell liquidity by reducing cash balances should be analyzed in the same way any other investment decision is analyzed. Management should project the future cash receipts and cash payments of the firm with various cash balances, subtract the payments from the receipts to determine *net* cash flows, and then select that cash balance (i.e., purchase that amount of liquidity) which maximizes the present value of the net cash flows.

An increase in cash balances is therefore considered to be a purchase of liquidity and is defined as a cash payment. A reduction in cash balances is a sale of liquidity and is defined as a cash receipt. If a firm receives cash from the sale of a product and increases its bank balance, the actions involve both a cash receipt and a cash payment, so that the net cash flow is zero. Subsequently, when the firm reduces its bank balance to pay wages, again the action involves both a cash receipt and a cash payment, with a net cash flow of zero.

The net cash flow in any period, therefore, is the difference between cash received by the firm from purchasers, debtors, or banks and the cash used by the firm to increase cash balances, to pay for goods and services, to pay interest or repay debt, or to lend. Such flows must be associated with equity obligations — i.e., the net cash flow is the cash flow between the firm and its stockholders. A positive net cash flow represents a cash payment by the firm to the stockholders, such as a dividend payment or a stock repurchase, whereas a negative net cash flow represents a cash payment by the stockholders to the firm, that is, a new stock subscription.

The associated theory of stock valuation is based on three assumptions: first, that the cash receipts and the cash payments of the firm have been projected for each time period forever; [3] second, that there are no costs of transactions or flotation, or any costs other than interest (or dividends), involved in borrowing or repaying money or in buying or

[3] Since the net cash flows are between the firm and the stockholders, the time periods should, in principle, end whenever dividends are paid or new stock is issued. This would be somewhat awkward, since new shares are floated at irregular intervals that do not usually coincide with dividend payments. It is also clear that no significant error would be introduced by selecting an arbitrary time period, perhaps a year.

selling financial obligations; and third, that stockholders are indifferent about distinctions between capital gains and dividend income, so one can ignore problems that arise because of the different taxes on income and capital gains.

Cash-flow theory, then, says that the value of the stock is the present value of the future net cash flows.[4] This provides the justification for my treatment of cash balances. Cash flows can be defined to suit the purpose of the user, and the cash-flow concept will be most useful here if the flows are defined so that the present value of the net cash flows is the value of the stock. Since the stock value is logically the discounted value of the dividends, and not the value of the dividends plus the increase in cash balances, my somewhat peculiar treatment of cash balances is required.

Within the more usual context of investment decisions, a decision has a favorable influence on stock price if the present value of the net cash flows associated with the investment project is positive — i.e., if the firm could pay enough dividends to justify raising the necessary funds by a new issue of stock. If the net cash flows generated by the project are not used to pay dividends but are reinvested in the firm (perhaps to purchase liquidity), a second investment project is begun, and the two projects should be evaluated independently. The net cash flows associated with the second (reinvestment) project are negative and offset the positive net cash flow of the first project, so the net cash flow to the firm is zero. Since the peculiar treatment of cash balances does not arise in evaluating any decision except that about the level of cash balances themselves, my treatment of cash balances does not impair the usefulness of the cash-flow concept in investment decisions, and adds to its usefulness in stock valuation.

This theory implies that stockholders do not care whether the firm repurchases stock or pays dividends, since either action is a cash flow from the firm to the stockholder. This can be illustrated with a simple

[4] All dealings in the financial obligations of the firm could be excluded from the cash receipts and payments. The net cash flow would then include transactions with debt holders as well as stockholders. The present value of the net cash flows would be the total value of all the financial obligations of the firm, and the value of the stock would be the total value of the obligations less the value of the debt. This would be more in keeping with the stock valuation theory suggested by F. Modigliani and M. H. Miller in "The Cost of Capital, Corporation Finance and the Theory of Investment," *American Economic Review*, XLVIII (June 1958), 261–297 (also reprinted in Solomon).

example. Suppose that a firm has 100 shares outstanding and is going to return $2,500 to stockholders. The value of the firm after the money has been distributed, which one can assume to be $10,000, is the discounted value of the net cash flows after that date and is not influenced by the way the funds are returned to the stockholders. If the stockholders expect a $25 dividend per share, each shareholder, subsequent to the dividend distribution, will have a share worth $100 and a $25 dividend. Before the dividend is paid, therefore, the shares must be valued at $125.

The shares must also be valued at $125 if the firm is expected to use the $2,500 to repurchase stock rather than to pay dividends, since the price of each share must be the same before and after the stock repurchase. If the shares are worth $125 before the purchase, the company can purchase twenty shares for $2,500. The stockholders who sell will receive $125 per share; each share still outstanding will represent one eightieth of the total stock (which still has a total value of $10,000) and therefore will be valued at $125.[5] In short, if the firm returns $2,500 to them, the stockholders do not care whether the firm declares cash dividend or whether the firm buys a given proportion of each stockholder's shares. Each stockholder owns the same proportion of the shares outstanding and receives the same amount of cash.[6]

This theory has some interesting implications with respect to future investment projects, future financing decisions, and future dividend payments. The emphasis on dividend payments might be misinterpreted to mean that dividend policy is important in determining stock value. This is not the case. If a firm has decided to undertake an investment project which involves the outlay of, say, $1 million, it makes no difference whether the money is obtained by reducing dividends or is paid out in dividends and then borrowed by issuing new stock.

The net cash flows that determine the stock value have been defined as the flows between the firm and its stockholders, and these flows are not changed by the decision to finance internally or to issue new stock. If the stockholders receive a dividend of $1 million, this is a net cash flow of plus $1 million. If $1 million of new stock is sold, this is a net

[5] This proof follows the pattern used by M. H. Miller and F. Modigliani in "Dividend Policy, Growth, and the Valuation of Shares," *Journal of Business*, XXXIV (October 1961), 411–433.

[6] This, of course, relies on the assumptions that there are no costs of transactions and that stockholders are indifferent between capital gains and dividend income.

cash flow of minus $1 million. If both transactions take place in the same period, the net cash flow is the sum of the two, or zero. This is, however, exactly what the net cash flow would be if no dividends were paid, no new stock were issued, and the project were financed internally.[7]

The theory also implies that a decision to undertake investment projects in the future influences the value of the stock today. The stock value is based entirely upon future cash flows, and it makes no difference whether the flows are expected in connection with a project already undertaken or one to be undertaken in the future.[8] It makes no difference, that is, unless the cash flows associated with future projects are considered to be more risky than those associated with current projects and therefore are discounted at a higher rate. The determination of the appropriate rate at which to discount future cash flows, sometimes called the normal rate of return on investment, is, unfortunately, beyond the scope of this paper.

THE CASH-FLOW CONCEPT OF PROFIT

Profit is defined in connection with a particular time period and reflects some of the activities of the firm during the period. I shall first consider three concepts relating to the status of the firm at the beginning and end of the period.

Stockholders' Initial Investment. This is the market value of the stock at the beginning of the period. It is the stockholders' initial investment in the sense that it represents what the stockholders could get by selling their shares at the beginning of the period, and is thus the amount of their wealth which they have entrusted to the firm for the period. Symbolically, the theory says:

$$S_0 = \frac{N_1}{(1+r)} + \frac{N_2}{(1+r)^2} + \frac{N_3}{(1+r)^3} + \cdots = \sum_{i=1}^{\infty} \frac{N_i}{(1+r)^i}$$

where S_0 = stock value at the start of the period (stockholders' initial

---

[7] For a more complete discussion of the influence of dividend policy on stock valuation, see Miller and Modigliani, "Dividend Policy."

[8] For further discussion of this point, see Armen Alchian, "Costs and Outputs," in Moses Abramovitz *et al.*, *The Allocation of Economic Resources, Essays in Honor of Bernard Francis Haley* (Stanford, Calif.: Stanford University Press, 1959); Bodenhorn, "On the Problem of Capital Budgeting"; and Miller and Modigliani, "Dividend Policy."

investment); $N_1, N_2 \ldots =$ net cash flows expected in future periods; and $r =$ discount rate.[9]

Stockholders' Expected End-of-Period Wealth. At the start of the period, the stockholders expect that their initial investment will yield a return during the period. Their expected end-of-period wealth, $E(W_1)$, consists of the expected net cash flow of the period, N_1, plus the expected end-of-period stock value:

$$E(W_1) = N_1 + \frac{N_2}{(1+r)} + \frac{N_3}{(1+r)^2} + \ldots =$$

$$\sum_{i=1}^{\infty} \frac{N_i}{(1+r)^{i-1}} = S_0(1+r)$$

This means that the expected return during the period is the normal rate of return on the initial investment as given by the discount rate.

Stockholders' Actual End-of-Period Wealth. This is the cash flow that actually takes place during the period, C_1, plus the actual stock value at the end of the period, i.e., the investment that the stockholders carry over into the next period, S_1.

$$W_1 = C_1 + S_1 = C_1 + \frac{M_2}{(1+r)} + \frac{M_3}{(1+r)^2} + \ldots =$$

$$C_1 + \sum_{i=2}^{\infty} \frac{M_i}{(1+r)^{i-1}}$$

where $W_1 =$ end-of-period wealth; $C_1 =$ actual cash flow of period; $S_1 =$ stock value at end of period $=$ investment carried forward to next period; and $M_2, M_3 \ldots =$ net cash flows expected in future periods.

Actual wealth can differ from expected wealth for any of three reasons: the cash flow of the period is different from what had been expected ($C_1 \neq N_1$); the cash flows expected in future periods have changed since the start of the period ($M_i \neq N_i$); or the discount rate has changed. In a world of certainty where expectations always come true and never change, actual wealth would be the same as expected wealth and would increase from period to period by the discount rate multiplied by the initial investment.

Pure Profit. The economist usually defines pure profit as a return in

[9] I shall assume throughout that this rate is determined in the market, but shall not seek to explain how it is determined.

excess of the normal return on invested capital — in this case the discount rate, since the normal return is regarded as a cost. The corresponding cash-flow definition is the difference between actual and expected end-of-period wealth. Thus, pure profit $= W_1 - E(W_1) = W_1 - S_0(1 + r)$.

Business Profit or Income. Businessmen and accountants usually look upon the entire return to stockholders as profit or income, and do not regard any part of return as a cost. Thus, business profit is pure profit plus the normal return on investment, which is also the difference between end-of-period wealth and initial investment, or, business profit $= W_1 - S_0 =$ pure profit $+ rS_0$. If expectations for the period are fulfilled ($N_1 = C_1$), future expectations unchanged ($M_1 = N_1$), and the discount rate unchanged, then pure profit is zero and business profit is the normal return on initial investment, rS_0.

The decisions of management during the period will be in the best interests of its stockholders if they maximize end-of-period wealth, business profit, or pure profit. These three criteria are logically equivalent because wealth, business profit, and pure profit differ by values that depend upon the initial expectations but cannot change during the period. End-of-period wealth and business profit differ by the initial stock value or investment, and business profit and pure profit differ by the normal return on the initial investment.

This concept of profit is significantly different from the conventional concept, which I shall call "earnings" so that the word "profit" can be reserved for the cash-flow concept. Earnings of a period are associated with the difference between the sales value and the cost of production of the goods sold [10] during the period; they are therefore concerned primarily with activity during the period. Earlier and later periods are involved only to the extent that expenses associated with current sales are paid in other periods or revenues associated with current sales are received in other periods. Earnings are not influenced by changed expectations about the future as profits are.

The differences between the use of cash-flow profit and the traditional use of earnings can be illustrated by considering the analysis of a simple investment project. The project requires a capital outlay of $1,000 at the beginning of the first year. At the end of the first year, the

---

[10] Sometimes the goods produced are considered but this would not affect the argument in this paper.

firm will receive $1,120 in sales revenue and will pay $400 in wages and $60 in corporate income taxes, and at the end of the second year, it will receive $1,310 in sales revenue and will pay $500 in wages and $205 in corporate income taxes. The income taxes are calculated by charging $600 of depreciation expenses the first year and $400 the second, which I assume the tax laws to permit. A tax rate of 50 per cent is then applied to taxable income (revenue minus wages minus depreciation) of $120 the first year and $410 the second. No other receipts or payments are associated with the project.

The project therefore has a net cash flow of —$1,000 at the start of the first year, +$660 at the end of the first year, and +$605 at the end of the second year. If we assume a discount rate of 10 per cent, the present (start of first year) value of the net cash flow is +$100 for the project.

It is easier to see the implications of the cash-flow analysis of this project with its associated profit and stock values if we assume that an entrepreneur incorporates solely for the purpose of engaging in this project and that the project is equity financed. Indeed, equity financing has already been assumed by the net cash flow of —$1,000 when the asset is purchased. By definition, a net cash flow is a transaction with stockholders, and the negative sign implies a flow of cash from the stockholders to the firm.[11] The analysis would not be changed in any important way if we assumed this project to be an addition to a going concern. It would become more complicated, however, since it might be financed internally — i.e., the funds to buy the asset might be obtained from cash receipts generated by other projects, and the receipts from the project might be used to finance other projects instead of being returned to stockholders. The principles are clearer, but not different, if we assume that the firm and the project coincide, so that cash flows generated by the project are also net cash flows to the firm.

The simplest case to consider is one in which the investment project was not anticipated by the market, but the market adopts the forecast by the firm of its future net cash flows immediately when the asset is purchased.[12] The sequence of events follows: (1) An entrepreneur

---

[11] I shall discuss below some of the problems which arise if the project is partly debt financed.

[12] Complications arise if the market delays in adopting the forecasts of the firm or has anticipated the project in the case of a going concern, but again there is no difference in principle.

takes $1,000 of his own money and buys an asset with the expectation that he can get a net cash flow of $660 at the end of the first year and $605 at the end of the second. (2) He incorporates and issues stock to himself at the same time that he buys the asset. (3) The market values this stock at $1,100 when it is issued because this is the present value of the expected future cash flows, discounted at 10 per cent. (4) The entrepreneur therefore makes a capital gain of $100 at the time that he issues the stock since he has paid $1,000 for the asset and has stock he could liquidate for $1,100. This increase in his wealth takes place whether or not he actually sells the stock, and is his "initial investment" in the firm according to my definitions. It is also a business profit and a pure profit, received at the start of the first year, since his actual wealth is $1,100, and his expected (by the market) wealth had been $1,000. (5) If all goes as expected, the firm returns $660 to its stockholders (who may or may not include the original entrepreneur) at the end of the first year. If the expectations for the second year are unchanged, the stockholders also have stock valued at $550, which is the present (start of second year) value of the cash flow of $605 expected at the end of the year. The stockholders' actual end-of-period wealth is $660 + $550 = $1,210, and *business profit* is $110 in the first year. *Pure profit* is zero, since the stockholders' normal rate of return of 10 per cent on their initial investment of $1,100 is also $110. (6) If expectations continue to be fulfilled, the firm returns $605 to its stockholders at the end of the second year, and the stock becomes worthless. End-of-period wealth is therefore $605. The initial investment for the second year is $550, since this is the stock value at the start of the year. *Business profit* is therefore $55, and *pure profit* is still zero.

Cash-flow theory says that all *pure* profit is earned when the stock value changes in a way that had not been anticipated by the market. The market value of the stock is always determined in such a way that the *expected* return (net cash flow – dividends – plus capital gains) is the *normal* return on the market value at the start of the period. If all goes as expected, the actual return, *business* profit, will be the expected normal return, and *pure* profit will be zero. If expectations change, a *pure* profit (or loss) is made immediately because the price of the stock makes an unexpected adjustment so that the newly expected future returns will equal a normal return on the new stock value (investment).

Analysis of the project within the context of traditional theory about earnings requires information about *economic* depreciation that cash-flow analysis does not require. Cash-flow analysis requires information only about corporate income taxes, which requires knowledge about legal but not about economic depreciation.[13] Although there is some debate, particularly among accountants, about the precise meaning of economic depreciation, I shall define it as the change in the market value of the asset.[14] We can also assume, for the time being, that legal depreciation and economic depreciation are the same — i.e., that the asset has a value of $400 at the end of the first year. Traditional earnings analysis then says that the firm raises $1,000 in capital at the start of the first year. It earns (net of taxes) $60 the first year. Since it returns $660 at the end of the year, $600 of this represents a return of capital, and the stockholders still have $400 invested. Earnings in the second year are $205. The $605 paid to stockholders at the end of the year represents a disbursement of the earnings and a full return of the $400 investment.

The cash-flow and earnings analyses are summarized in the table, where cash-flow analysis shows an immediate capital gain of $100, with

Cash-Flow and Earnings Analyses of a Firm
for a Two-Year Period

Kind of Analysis	Start of 1st Year	End of 1st Year	End of 2nd Year
Cash-flow			
Business profit	$ 100	$110	$ 55
Pure profit	100	0	0
Stockholders' investment	1,100	550	0
Earnings			
Earnings	0	60	205
Pure earnings [a]	0	−40	165
Stockholders' investment	1,000	400	0

[a] This concept is discussed in the next section, "The Problem of Depreciation."

[13] Another way of looking at this is to observe that no depreciation calculation would be required for cash-flow analysis if there were no income tax, whereas depreciation would still be required for earnings analysis.

[14] This definition has the advantage of being tied to market values, and so is unambiguously measurable after the fact. There is no other definition of depreciation, except one tied to cash flows in such a way that earnings and business profit become identical, which is not subject to the same criticisms I am about to make of this concept of depreciation.

subsequent business profit of a normal 10 per cent on investment and with no pure profit. Earnings analysis shows no immediate capital gain and earnings of 6 per cent on investment the first year and 51.25 per cent the second.

I shall now discuss reasons for preferring the cash-flow approach.

THE PROBLEM OF DEPRECIATION

The fundamental criticism of the treatment of depreciation in earnings analysis is that the economic depreciation expense understates the capital costs. The actual cost is $1,000 at the start of the first year, and the depreciation expenses over the two years add (undiscounted) to $1,000. The present (start of first year) value of the depreciation expenses is therefore less than the actual cost of $1,000.[15]

The solution to this problem, within the framework of earnings analysis, is to charge an implicit interest expense on the book value of the stockholders' investment (net worth) at the normal rate of return, 10 per cent. In the case of equity financing, which I have been considering, this is equivalent to charging implicit interest on the undepreciated asset balance.[16] However, if the asset is financed in whole or in part by debt,[17] on which interest is included explicitly, costs would be overstated if an implicit interest expense were included on the entire undepreciated asset balance.

The inclusion of implicit interest on net worth makes the present

[15] This criticism also applies to long-run static equilibrium where depreciation just covers replacement in each period so that the initial investment never gets charged as an expense. Let the initial investment be I, with annual replacement of R. The present value of the investment plus replacement is therefore $I + R/r$. If the annual depreciation charge is D, the present value of the depreciation charges is D/r. In the long-run static equilibrium $D = R$, and the true cost of the investment, $I + R/r$, exceeds the present value of the depreciation expenses by the initial investment, I.

[16] This suggestion was made by Edgar O. Edwards and Philip W. Bell in *The Theory and Measurement of Business Income* (Berkeley and Los Angeles: University of California Press, 1961), p. 68.

[17] This, of course, would change the net cash flows. In the example, if $500 is raised by borrowing, the net cash flow at the start of the first year is only −$500. There is a cash payment of $1,000 for the asset, and a cash receipt of $500 from debt holders. Only $500 is raised from stockholders, and this is the net cash flow. The net cash flows would be reduced in subsequent periods also, because debt repayment and interest are cash payments which must be subtracted from the cash receipts to get the net cash flows (to stockholders). The debt financing might also raise the discount rate on the equity return (net cash flow), but I continue to assume that the appropriate discount rate, as influenced by the debt issue, is known.

(start of first year) value of the costs charged to equity capital in each year — depreciation minus debt repayment plus implicit interest — equal to the initial equity investment.[18] Since the present value of the debt repayment and associated interest expenses must equal the initial debt investment, all capital charges are accounted for.

Pure earnings can now be defined as earnings minus implicit interest, and pure earnings then account for all capital costs. In the example, the book value of the stockholders' investment is $1,000 at the start of the first year and $400 at the start of the second, so implicit interest would be $100 the first year and $40 the second, and pure earnings would be —$40 the first year and $165 the second. The fact that the pure earnings account for capital costs means that the present (start of first year) value of the pure earnings is the same as the present value of the net cash flows, which also account for all capital costs.[19] Cash-

[18] Consider a case in which the net cash flows are N_0 at the start of the first year, N_1 at the end of the year, and N_2 at the end of the second year. Bonds (B) are issued at the start of the first year, of which B_1 are due at the end of the first year and $B - B_1$ at the end of the second year. The initial asset value is $A = B - N_0$, since we raise N_0 from stockholders. Depreciation is D_1 the first year and $A - D_1$ the second year. The book value of the net worth is $-N_0$ at the start of the first year, so the implicit interest charge is $-rN_0$. The firm returns N_1 to its stockholders at the end of the first year, of which $N_1 - D_1 + B_1$ represent earnings and $D_1 - B_1$ represent a return of capital. Book value of net worth is therefore $-N_0 - D_1 + B_1$ at the end of the first year, and implicit interest of $r(-N_0 - D_1 + B_1)$ must be charged in the second year. Charges (C) against equity capital are depreciation minus debt retirement plus implicit interest. So

$$C_1 = D_1 - B_1 - rN_0, \text{ and}$$
$$C_2 = A - D_1 - (B - B_1) + r(-N_0 - D_1 + B_1)$$
$$= A - B - rN_0 + (1 + r)(B_1 - D_1)$$
$$= -N_0 - rN_0 + (1 + r)(B_1 - D_1)$$
$$= (1 + r)(B_1 - D_1 - N_0)$$

The present (start of first year) value of these charges is

$$\frac{C_1}{1+r} + \frac{C_2}{(1+r)^2} = \frac{D_1 - B_1 - rN_0}{1+r} + \frac{(B_1 - D_1 - N_0)(1+r)}{(1+r)^2}$$
$$= \frac{D_1 - B_1 - rN_0 + B_1 - D_1 - N_0}{(1+r)}$$
$$= -N_0$$

[19] Since the discount rate is 10 per cent,

$$\frac{-40}{1.1} + \frac{165}{1.21} = \frac{-44}{1.21} + \frac{165}{1.21} = \frac{121}{1.21} = 100$$

More generally, using the notation of the last footnote, and denoting the pure earnings by P_1 and P_2,

$$P_1 = N_1 - D_1 + B_1 + rN_0$$

flow analysis accounts for these costs much more simply, however, by charging the cost as a cash payment when the asset is bought. Depreciation and implicit interest need not be considered, since they do not give rise to cash flows.

THE PROBLEM OF MAXIMIZATION

The correct calculation of capital costs is necessary for decision-making — this means that the maximization of earnings is not in the stockholders' interest, but the maximization of *pure* earnings is.

The maximization of earnings can be misleading even in the determination of the output rate by setting marginal cost equal to marginal revenue in the framework of comparative statics. In this case, the marginal revenue is the same as the marginal cash receipts, and marginal cost is the marginal cash payment, so the difference between marginal revenue and marginal cost is the marginal net cash flow. Since a positive marginal net cash flow necessarily increases the present value of the future net cash flows and so increases profits, cash-flow theory confirms the traditional result that output should be increased if marginal revenue exceeds marginal cost.

This is true, however, only if revenues and costs both increase at the same time. If the cost increases first and some time elapses before the product is sold and revenue increases, then the cash outlay during this interval of time must be regarded as an investment in the context of earnings analysis and as a net cash payment in cash-flow analysis. Earnings will rise if marginal revenue exceeds marginal cost, but the output should be increased only if the difference is large enough to provide a normal rate of return on the additional (equity) investment; therefore, earnings maximization is an inadequate criterion for decisions. Cash-flow analysis gives the correct result by requiring that the present value

$$
\begin{aligned}
P_2 &= N_2 - (A - D_1) + (B - B_1) - r(-N_0 - D_1 + B_1) \\
&= N_2 - A + B + rN_0 - (1 + r)(B_1 - D_1) \\
&= N_2 + N_0 + rN_0 - (1 + r)(B_1 - D_1) \\
&= N_2 - (1 + r)(B_1 - D_1 - N_0)
\end{aligned}
$$

The present (start of first year) value is

$$
\frac{P_1}{1+r} + \frac{P_2}{(1+r)^2} = \frac{N_1 - D_1 + B_1 + rN_0}{1+r} + \frac{N_2}{(1+r)^2} - \frac{B_1 - D_1 - N_0}{(1+r)}
$$

$$
= N_0 + \frac{N_1}{1+r} + \frac{N_2}{(1+r)^2}
$$

of the future net cash receipts generated when the marginal revenue exceeds marginal cost be at least as large as the present value of the net cash payments generated after the marginal cost has risen but before the marginal revenue has risen.

An example related to the investment project discussed in the preceding two sections will also illuminate some of the problems. Suppose that a firm must select either that project or an alternative project with identical cash flows [20] but with economic depreciation of $500 in each of the two years. Such a project would be indistinguishable from the first when one uses cash-flow analysis. Earnings analysis, however, would show earnings of $160 the first year (instead of $60 as the original project) and of $105 the second (instead of $205). Pure earnings would be $60 the first year (instead of −$40) and $55 the second (instead of $165). Maximization of earnings would lead to selecting the alternative project, since it earns $100 more the first year and $100 less the second. Maximization of pure earnings, however, leads again to the conclusion that the projects are equally profitable since the present value of the pure earnings is $100 for either.

This is not a coincidence and illustrates an important point. The present value of the pure earnings of a project does not depend in any way on the pattern of economic depreciation, even though this economic depreciation is charged as an expense in the various periods. We have already seen (in footnote 19) that the present value of the pure earnings equals the present value of the net cash flows, and the pattern of economic depreciation influences neither the net cash flows nor their present value.

The conclusion is that maximization of earnings is not an appropriate criterion for decisions unless the earnings are corrected for implicit interest on the book value of the net worth to obtain pure earnings. However, the present value of the pure earnings is independent of the pattern of depreciation, and it therefore seems hardly worthwhile to go to the trouble of determining depreciation and the implicit interest charge. It is simpler (but logically the same) to maximize the present value of the net cash flows.

[20] This implies that the tax payments are the same for the two projects and that they have the same tax depreciation. This is necessary if one is to distinguish the impact of economic depreciation from the impact of tax depreciation. For further discussion of this point see Bodenhorn, "Depreciation."

Profits in the Modern Economy

The only possible advantages of pure earnings over cash-flow profit would be either that they give more accurately the timing of the benefits from the investment project or that they are easier to measure at the end of the period.

With respect to timing, cash-flow theory says that the original project creates a pure profit of $100 at the start of the first year and in the two years thereafter earns only a normal profit of 10 per cent on investment. Earnings theory says that there are no pure earnings at the start of the first year and that the return on investment during the first year falls short of a normal 10 per cent by $40 (pure earnings of —$40) and during the second exceeds a normal 10 per cent by $165. Since the present (start of first year) value of the pure earnings is the same as the present value of the pure profit, the dispute is really about the timing of the realization of the pure profit or earnings and not about the total amount involved.

The approaches agree in defining pure profit as the ordinary profit (herein called business profit) or earnings less a normal return on invested capital. They differ in measurements both of the ordinary profit or earnings and of the amount of invested capital.[21] If we adopt the strongest version of traditional theory and take assets at their market value so that depreciation is the change in market value, then both cash-flow and traditional theory base their measurements of profit (or earnings) and invested capital upon market values. Earnings are associated with the potential (but usually hypothetical) sale of the assets of the firm at market value. Cash-flow profit is associated with the potential (but usually hypothetical) sale of the equities of the firm at market value.

Traditional earnings are the difference between the book value of the net worth at the end of the year and its book value at the beginning of the year, plus the net cash flow. They are associated with asset values because the net worth is the residual after debt is subtracted from the market value of the assets. They therefore show the gains accruing to the stockholder because the firm refrained from selling its assets at

[21] I am assuming that they agree in their measurement of the normal rate of return, although this is not necessarily the case.

114

market for an additional year.[22] Cash-flow business profit is the difference between the market value of the stock at the end of the year and its market value at the beginning of the year, also plus the net cash flow. It therefore shows the income accruing to stockholders because they held their stock for an additional year, if income is defined in the usual way as "the maximum possible consumption without reducing wealth."

The traditional approach is to measure the stockholders' investment as the book value of the net worth, which is the appropriate base in the determination of implicit interest. Cash-flow theory measures the stockholders' investment as the market value of the firm's stock.

This difference in the measurement of stockholders' investment extends to the analysis of static equilibrium, where there is no difference between earnings and business profit. In static equilibrium, the liquidation value of the assets, the book value of net worth, and the market value of the stock must be the same at the start and the end of the year. Both earnings and business profit therefore equal the net cash flow. Nevertheless, traditional theory says a monopoly earns a pure profit because its revenues exceed its costs — including as a cost implicit interest on net worth. Cash-flow theory says no pure profit can exist in static equilibrium because nothing unexpected ever happens. The pure profit of traditional theory gets capitalized in the form of a higher stock price when the market registers that the monopoly has been obtained. At that time the stockholders' investment increases by just enough to eliminate any pure profit beyond the normal return on investment.

The advantage of cash-flow theory does not lie in the fact that it considers the potential sale of equities rather than of assets. Indeed, cash-flow theory says that it makes no difference whether assets or equities are sold, provided the assets are sold together as a going concern rather than piecemeal at market value. That is, cash-flow theory says that the value of the assets as a going concern is the present value of the net cash flows and also that this is the value the market should place on the stock. Thus, sale of the firm as a going concern will yield the same return to stockholders they could get by selling their stock. The mistake of the traditional analysis is considering the sale of the assets piecemeal at a price less than the maximum obtainable. Calcula-

[22] This concept of earnings, based on valuing assets at market, has been called "realizable profit" by Edwards and Bell, pp. 44ff.

tions of earnings should not be based on the assumption that management would so blunder.

The effect of considering sale in the wrong market at too low a price is that earnings bear no relation to stockholders' returns — stockholders can be making money on their stock when the firm is losing money (and vice versa). The separation of the earnings of the firm from those of the stockholders serves no useful purpose. Business profit is always the same as stockholders' income and its maximization is always in the stockholders' interest. Cash-flow theory also says that the allocation of the pure profit of $100 to subsequent years as pure earnings is unnecessary since the stockholders get income in the form of capital gain when the pure profit is recorded.

THE PROBLEM OF MEASUREMENT

If the objective of the firm is to earn a profit for its stockholders, the amount of profit earned during a period can be used as a criterion in measuring the performance of the firm. It is therefore desirable to have a profit concept measurable on the basis of market values and thus objective in the accounting sense.

Of the four profit concepts considered in this paper, two — business profit and earnings [23] — are measurable from market data. Neither pure earnings nor pure profit is so measurable because both require use of the normal rate of return — not directly observable in the market. Maximization of earnings is not in the stockholders' interest and hence is not a satisfactory measure of performance. This leaves business profit as the only satisfactory measure of performance.

---

[23] Earnings are measurable if, as I have been assuming, assets are carried on the books at market value. Otherwise there is likely to be a dispute about the objectivity of the depreciation calculation.

FRANCIS M. BODDY

A Pragmatic View of Profit

I SHALL begin by stating my biases and reason for proposing that profits can be looked at in a couple of different ways. This will be inconclusive, but it may put a little order back into what I am afraid Professor Nelson completely disordered when he said there were so many things wrong with any specific kind of measurement of profit.

First, I would like to say "amen" to Nelson's main point, which I take to be that any figure with a name attached to it, such as profit, is going to be used by a variety of people for a variety of purposes. It is, in a sense, an all-purpose statistic and, like most all-purpose statistics, seldom answers very well the specific question in which one is interested.

My biases arise from two interests: First, as an economist, I am chiefly interested in the process of decision-making. I look at accounting information, whatever labels are attached to it, basically as information to be manipulated, built into models, or analyzed for the purpose of making decisions. I am primarily a microeconomist, and so I concentrate upon decision-making within the firm, the effect of the decisions on markets, and the subsequent effect of market structures back upon decision makers. Second, I teach a course on the Russian economy. The Soviets are struggling with exactly the same problem — namely, the appropriate measure of profits. They also are looking for a single-purpose index which they can use to control, manage, or measure the performance of the enterprise in a system which is completely different from and yet has the same problems of checking performance as ours.

If performance indicators — or, as people interested in this topic usually call them, "success indicators" — are aggregated into a single

117

index, the weights are likely to be somewhat arbitrary, resulting in a great dilemma. The Russians for a long time laid down a list of success indicators, each one of which was supposed to be met by the executor of the plan. The plan was very detailed, giving gross output, and output by size, class, color, and so on. This is one kind of measure of success in the Russian planning system.

Troubles with this plan led to a second, now being developed. The more specific and detailed these plans are, the harder it is to fulfill them, and the harder it is to fulfill them, the more cheating goes on. Thus if the plan calls for the output of a certain tonnage of castings in a casting plant, there is a tremendous incentive to make big castings because they are easier and cheaper to make and fulfill the plan in tonnage.

What the Russians call the problem of assortment — the enforcement of very detailed specifications of all kinds of output — has been bothering them for many years. Now it is becoming even more troublesome as the productive processes become more complex, the economy larger, and interrelations between enterprises more elaborate.

And so the Russian economists and engineers (it really started among the engineers, rather than the economists, which I believe is typical in many countries) raised questions about the falsity or utility of the kinds of planning procedures and indicators being used. This generated further discussions, leading to the attempt to create an all-purpose index that I shall call "profits." These Soviet technicians are, undoubtedly, going to define these profits somewhat differently than we should. That is, while their definition of profit is the same as ours, their concept of revenue is somewhat different, and their concept of cost is even more different because they don't recognize, for example, capital cost in any real sense, or land cost at all because of the dogma of the system.

Let me suggest, then, that perhaps one way a business firm can use the figure we have customarily called profit is as a success indicator. The size of the profit is a measure of success, but profit is undefined until the process by which it is measured is defined. I believe strongly in operational definitions — it becomes almost meaningless to talk about profits unless one specifies the process by which the thing called profits is to be measured. It is all right to talk about profit in some philosophical sense as a concept or idea, but when it comes down to handling it pragmatically in decision-making, it is important that one be able to

118

attach numerical values to it and also that those numerical values be cardinal rather than ordinal — that is, that a profit of $2,000 is twice $1,000, rather than just bigger.

One way of looking at profits, then, is to consider them as a measure of the success of a business enterprise, and then ask what kind of success indicator we would like to have. The difficulty is that we can set up simple, quite defensible measures that lead to a persuasive definition of profit if we restrict ourselves to simple cases and particularly avoid the case in which unpredictable change seems to be the best prediction to make. Predictable change is risk and is statistically handleable in at least a middling fashion. Unpredictable change is what upsets so much of measurement. This is particularly true, of course, of accounting conventions regarding the cost of fixed assets purchased in one period and used over a long life. Professor Hunt's paper suggests that our real interest in the past is only as a forecast of the future.

Suppose we suggest that in order to define profits, we must define what the stockholders would like to instruct managers to maximize, if there is a single thing. Then make this as big as possible. This is, in general, the way economists have always looked at profits. They have looked at them, I grant, in a very specialized set of cases, with most discussions in terms of certainty, avoiding abstractions from the real world.

The effectiveness of economics, I believe, has been that in spite of those abstractions, we are nevertheless helped to understand and to make predictions about the real world — not so well as we'd like to, but better than the predictions of non-economists with the same kind of information.

What should the stockholders instruct the management to measure? And how should it be measured to judge the performance of management? I sympathize with the view (abstracting the capital gains feature of the income tax) that the objective of management ought to be to maximize the total dividends plus the value of the stock at the end of the period. This still leaves the choice as to which of these things ought to be maximized in the long run, but if one assumes that the market gives the correct value, in some sense, of the assets of the firm, the market value of the equity interests at the end of the year plus dividends received during the year less the market value of the equity at the beginning of the year would seem to be a fairly sensible single figure.

119

Profits in the Modern Economy

The problem is to devise a system of measurement which will do that, and the solution turns out to be easy: get the market values, and then keep a record of the dividends received by the stockholders. I believe there is some argument about what stockholders really want, but this is largely owing to the impact of the capital gains tax. If it were not for the capital gains tax, it wouldn't really matter to me as a stockholder whether the value of my stock goes up $10 a year and I get no dividends, or I get $10 a year and the value of the stock stays constant. I can always sell stock if I need money, and I can always put my money back in again if I don't wish to spend the dividend. There is a great persuasive value in the choice of these measures. Of course this isn't what accountants are used to, and certainly this figure is badly distorted at the present time by the unwillingness of stockholders to exercise this choice. In other words, because much extraneous information (such as earnings per share and a variety of other things of this sort) is furnished them, and because it is accounted for in great detail and guaranteed by certified public accountants, stockholders believe the information has something to do with the figures they *ought* to be looking at.

When one comes to the fact that there is special taxation of capital gains in our system, I'd agree pretty much with the position Professor Hunt takes. For example, knowing the kind of stockholders, their income tax brackets, and the effect on them of capital gains versus regular income taxes, one could set up a success indicator for the management of that particular concern. But what is this "success" compared to? (This is like the famous story about the man on the street who asks a man he meets, "How is your wife?" The other retorts, "Compared to what?")

Success is usually a comparative concept, but not always. Herbert Simon has been pushing the idea that success to some means merely a satisfactory level, not necessarily the maximum possible. Yet the whole argument of the incentive of profit in our economic system is an attempt to maximize. If the system is not maximizing, it is either because people aren't under the competitive pressure that economists think they are or because their real interests are not the things being measured by this "profit" they are not maximizing. It used to be said that people aren't maximizing profits because, obviously, the way they do things in some circumstances is not maximizing behavior. An outstanding example of

120

this occurred shortly after World War II. The automobile industry — that is, manufacturers — was quite obviously not maximizing profits because, in the black market, many dealers were receiving anywhere from $200 to $500 above list price, a profit that could have been seized by manufacturers. This was said to illustrate that economists who talk about profits as something to maximize are not operationally in tune with businessmen. But when one looks at the labor situation of manufacturers at that time, it is plausible to argue that it didn't pay to maximize in the short run because this would have encouraged demands for greater wages. Manufacturers were, in effect, maximizing something measured by "profits" in the long run.

The accounting of profits is cluttered by the accountant's conservative tendency to record costs on a historical basis rather than at current prices. But even this is arguable. For example, suppose there is an industry in which demand is declining and in which, therefore, no new investment is taking place. It has long-lived assets with the capacity to satisfy the present demand, and, in addition, demand is declining no faster than assets are wearing out. The current cost of replacing these assets has nothing to do with the market price at all, since they are not being replaced. Market price is not established at a margin estimated by the cost of new plant, and so it would seem to me that historical cost in this case is possibly as good as current cost for accounting of profit.

On the other hand, if an industry is expanding and if it has a large amount of old capital now in use, then historical cost will show these old plants to be producing very large profits indeed, because prices will have to be sufficient to support investment in much more expensive new plants. The manager may be patting himself on the back for the high profits he had nothing to do with. So historical cost here is not really a useful performance index. But there isn't any single always-best performance index. The most we can expect is an index that does rough justice to the most important uses. People take different views because they have different criteria for what the most important interests are. If the chief interest is cost accounting, for example, and one is engaged in the present wave of managerial accounting, his view of costs is quite different from that of the financial accountant brought up in the tradition of preserving the financial integrity of capital.

It comes to the point that, given our tax treatment of capital gain versus dividend income, I'd heartily endorse the suggestion that the most useful single figure would be one that counted after-tax profits plus the after-tax recoverable amount of capital gain as profit. But since this would vary among stockholders, what might be called the current accounting practice would not be current accounting practice any more but a variety of different practices in the sense, at least, of giving different numbers in different circumstances. But in the case of a large, publicly held company, then I believe something could be said for a single index.

My major argument is that it is almost impossible to answer a specific question on the basis of a measure designed for some other purpose. Therefore, the hope that we can get real agreement is, I believe, a false one. There just is no way of getting a consistently useful measure of profits that will satisfy the needs of all users of the figure. The important thing is to give much more information about the measurement than is being used and not simply to attach a name to the answer. The reader is likely to assume that everything labeled "profit" is discovered by the same process of measurement. But, as Nelson has demonstrated, the process of measurement can be consciously altered by management and by accountants to reach a variety of different objectives.

Ultimately, of course, the thing to do is not to issue any general purpose statistics but only special purpose statistics. Stockholders' reports ought to be geared to the family of stockholders in that particular company and ought to answer the questions most important to them. The income tax law may define profit differently for tax purposes, and management may do what it can to avoid, legally, the impact of that tax by the way it presents its reports for the income tax. If the stockholders change, the process certainly should change, or it should at least take account of the new situation.

With respect to the general proposition, it seems to me that since profit is the incentive for investment, one should think of the investment interest in these firms. I believe the interest of the stockholder ought to dominate, at least in reporting his kind of profits. Basically — and I believe accountants in general would agree — the ideal which we can't possibly achieve would be to keep records in such a fashion that we could put together any report for any purpose. Our difficulty is that we are trying to apply a single process to and use a single measure for a wide variety of purposes; I see no hope of success in such an effort.

+ + +   HAROLD BIERMAN, Jr.

Investment Decisions of Corporations

INVESTMENT decisions of corporations are probably the single most important determinant of corporate profits which is directly controllable by corporations. They include the decisions of a firm about product line and the choice of equipment for producing the product. Decisions to buy or lease, or to make or buy, are investment decisions, as is the choice of the method of depreciation accounting. A firm deciding whether or not to refund a bond issue has an investment decision, and so does the president of a university deciding on the size of a new building for a school of business administration. All except the last decision will greatly affect the profits of a corporation.

Only a small fraction of the population will be financially interested in the profits of a specific corporation. However, in addition to the direct effect investment decisions have on the profits of the corporation making the investment, there are also indirect or macroeconomic effects, that is, the effects on the national economy.

There are few corporate executives who would suggest making an undesirable investment in order to sustain the national economy. However, each investment decision has its impact on the gross national product and indirectly affects the profits of other corporations. If an automobile company buys a machine tool, the profits of a machine tool company are increased, as are the profits of a steel company, a coal company, a public utility, a railroad, and so forth, and (at a different level of analysis) the employees of these companies buy from grocery stores, retail and mail order houses, and many other companies. An economist might describe this chain as a multiplier effect of an investment. It could be argued that the multiplier effect quickly tends to die out, but there remains another consideration. The investment generates product — one hopes more efficiently than its predecessors did — in the end making better and cheaper products that are more competitive in the world market, thus benefiting us all. (I am assuming that the problem of employment caused by automation is solvable. Unless the problem is solved, my statement concerning universal benefits would be more modest.) A person interested in economic development must be vitally interested in the processes of making investment decisions within corporations and governments, for investment decisions are among the most powerful and effective forces for improving the standard of living of man.

Several years ago in an address at Cornell about means for improving economic conditions of less developed countries, a speaker cited the benefits to be derived if American corporations invested in a particular Asian country. Living standards would be increased, and also the democratic institutions of the country would be strengthened in the battle against Communism. At that time the Asian country was actively discouraging investments by foreign corporations by restrictive controls and taxes considered by investors to create an unhealthy climate for investment. At no time did the speaker concede the necessity of attracting investment by offering opportunities that would satisfy the criteria for investment established by corporate managers in the interests of their stockholders. Now, it may be that these criteria are imperfect from the point of view of national interests, but a person interested in increasing the amount of investment in less developed areas cannot ignore them.

There is something we should say about the responsibilities of Americans toward less developed countries. It is disturbing that risks and lack of potential profit (at least on a comparative basis) will keep American corporations out of the very places that need their investments the most. I am suggesting that private corporations should assist in developing productive facilities in less developed countries. In each investment proposal for such a country there should be included a positive increment which I shall call "goodwill" and which represents the value of the investment to the people of the country which is host to the investment. Indirectly, this goodwill would return to the stockholders and other citizens of our country. I am arguing that less stringent, instead of more stringent, criteria should be applied in making the decisions that apply to such countries.

The idea is exciting, since it would involve exporting two of the most important possessions of the United States — industrial know-how and a workable free enterprise system — to the areas of the world in most need. Many investment opportunities now rejected by security-conscious, risk-avoiding corporations could be sought out and undertaken since the criteria for investment would be different. The objectives of the private corporation would be broadened to include raising the standard of living of those parts of the world that need this assistance the most. The corporations that follow this path may also be pleasantly surprised to find that there are also opportunities for profit being developed.

I turn now to the subject of how investment decisions are made in corporations. Studies made several years ago indicated that the four most widely used methods of making investment decisions are payback, return on investment, rate of return, and present value. I believe the relative popularity of the procedures would be somewhat different if the studies were made today, especially if the several methods were weighted by the amount of the investments made by each corporation. More and more of the large corporations have been switching to discounted cash-flow procedures and especially to the present-value method. In the academic literature of the last five years there has been little disagreement concerning the merits of the present-value method over the other known procedures. It may be helpful to review briefly here the merits and weaknesses of each procedure.

The payback procedure has the merits of being easy to understand and to compute — simply divide the investment by the cash return per year. Unfortunately, it has the damaging faults of not taking into consideration the life of the investment or the timing of the cash flows during the payback period. The critics of the payback procedure object to its use as a prime means of making investment decisions, although they do not object strenuously to its use as a supplemental means of describing an investment. It may be helpful in discussing the merits of an investment to add the information that it has a payback period of one year. However, it would be incorrect to eliminate an investment from consideration because its payback period is greater than x years and accept another investment because its payback period is less than x years. Fortunately, most of the leading business firms do not use the payback as the single criterion, but as a helpful guide.

Return on investment is sometimes called the "accounting method," though as an accountant, I prefer to call it the "other method." The procedure is to divide the average income earned over the life of the investment by the average (or the total) investment. It is implicitly hoped by the person making the computation that the percentage so obtained will be the same percentage produced by the accounting procedures once the investment is operating. Unfortunately, even if all the predictions came true, this would not hold. Only in a very special case would the return on investment obtained from the actual accounting information agree with the measure used to make the investment decision. In addition to this failure, the return-on-investment method also fails to incorporate into the analysis the time value of money. There is another difficulty, common to all ratios: a ratio or percentage — and return on investment is such a figure — cannot distinguish the size of the investment effectively, and hence may lead to an incorrect decision involving mutually exclusive investments (this may be called the scale problem).[1] The return-on-investment procedure as a criterion for investment is well entrenched in business usage and is likely to be used extensively for many years in the future.

The next two methods to be described may both be called discounted cash-flow procedures; they are the rate-of-return and the present-value methods.

The rate-of-return (or yield) procedure is a percentage that may be described in several ways: (1) it is the rate of discount which makes the present value of all cash flows equal to zero; (2) it is the highest rate at which funds may be borrowed to make the investment (assuming the cash flows from the investment are used to pay off the debt); and (3) it is the rate of growth of the investment.

The present-value procedure results in a measure of dollars showing the difference between the net present value of the future cash flows and outlays. In a sense, a positive net present value is the unrealized

---

[1] A mutually exclusive investment decision is one involving two or more investments, where only one will be chosen because of the nature of the process (only one type of heating plant is required for the building) or the physical nature of the investment (either a building or a baseball field can be built on a piece of land, not both). Two or more investments competing for the funds but otherwise independent are not mutually exclusive.

profit associated with the investment. It gives a measure of the profitability of the investment over and above the required profit on the investment, which has been taken into consideration by the use of a discount rate. The present-value method takes the time value of money into consideration by the use of a discount rate which represents the time value (or cost) of money to the firm. We may imagine the corporation asking itself, "What sum of money would have to be forthcoming x years from now for us to be indifferent when choosing between that sum and $1 now?" Frequently the rate of discount (commonly called the cost of capital) is determined by looking at the costs of the various sources of funds.

Both the rate-of-return and the present-value methods take the timing of the cash flows into consideration. The rate-of-return method implicitly assumes that the time value of money is equal to the rate of return. The present-value method implicitly assumes that the funds will be invested at the cost of capital. Both procedures will lead to the same decisions to accept or reject independent investments.[2] When one is using the rate-of-return procedure, if the rate of return is greater than the cost of capital, the investment should be accepted; if not, rejected. When one is using the present-value criterion, if the net present value of the cash flows is positive, the investment should be undertaken; if negative, the investment should be rejected.[3] Thus, in situations involving independent investments both of the discounted cash-flow procedures will lead to the same decisions to accept or reject and both effectively take the time value of money into consideration.

Now assume we have a set of mutually exclusive investments and we want to determine the best of the set. In this situation the rate-of-return criterion is inferior to the present-value procedure because although it can lead to the same choice if carefully used, it can also lead to incorrect decisions. Among the difficulties encountered — and

[2] The term "independent investment" is used to describe a collection of investments where there is no limitation on accepting all of the investments, except the possible financial limitation — i.e., the investment must justify the expenditure of funds. By definition, mutually exclusive investments are not independent.

[3] Some authors suggest that the present value of the positive cash flows should be divided by the investment outlays to obtain an index of present value. For independent investments, the index of present value will be greater than one when the net present value is positive and thus will lead to the same decisions to accept or reject. However, the advocates of this procedure make other, excessive claims for its use that are not warranted.

which become important in choosing the best of a set of mutually exclusive investments — are the scale problem (described above in discussion of the return on investment) and the fact that there may be more than one rate of return (one rate may indicate rejection and the other acceptance).

Although it is true that these difficulties may be overcome, the procedure does require considerable care. The net-present-value procedure may be used to choose the best of a set of mutually exclusive investments by applying the rule "choose the investment with the largest net present value." The one qualification (frequently not relevant) is that the lives of the investments be comparable, since we may not be able to compare two investments — one with a life of five years and one a life of two — without making their lives comparable.

Let us review what we can do. By the use of the discounted cash-flow procedures we can make decisions to accept or reject involving independent investments, and we can choose the best of a set of mutually exclusive investments. The literature of capital budgeting frequently discusses the ranking of independent investments. Except in the special situation involving clearly superior investments,[4] I do not know how to rank independent investments. I can choose the best of a set of mutually exclusive investments, but this is not the same as ranking of independent investments. Let us assume that I rank investments by using their rates of return. Immediately there is the problem of what to do about the funds generated. At what rate should they assume to be reinvested?[5] This is not a simple problem. If we use the net-present-value procedure to rank investments, we run into the problem of whether it is possible to combine or subdivide investments to change their ranking.

There is also the problem of what rate of discount to use. Assume we use the cost of capital to compute net present values and then choose the investment with the largest net present value, stating that it is the most desirable. There are other investments with positive net present values. The use of the cost of capital to compute the net pres-

---

[4] For example, given the following two independent investments, A is clearly superior to B, and we can rank A over B: at time zero, A and B both have cash flows of −$10,000; at time one, A earns $12,000 and B earns $11,000.

[5] For example, with a time value of money other than .10, the following two investments are not equally desirable even though they have the same rate of return: at time zero, A and B both have cash flows of −$10,000; at time one A earns $11,000 and at time two B earns $12,100.

ent value is no longer appropriate. The opportunity cost of funds to the firm is implicitly higher than the cost of capital.

If I were a financial executive asked by my superior to rank a set of independent investments, I could certainly give him a ranking. However, I should not like to try to defend it before a third person on the basis of the quantitative measures. Here again, I exclude the situation where there are clearly superior investments. It is possible to have investments that almost rank themselves, but in a realistic, complex situation in business this is rarely the case. I also exclude the state of affairs where there are so few investment opportunities in the present period and in future periods that I select a linear programing technique to make investment decisions.

Fortunately we can make a large percentage of investment decisions without ranking investments. In fact, unless a form of capital rationing is present, we do not have to rank the investments; rather, we can use the present-value method to make decisions to accept or reject. However, the problem of ranking does concern business executives, and I wish I could supply a simple answer, but I do not have one and know of no one who does.

I have frequently used the term "cash flows" in this paper, meaning the essential inputs of the payback and the discounted cash-flow procedures. The easiest and most direct method of explaining cash flow is to consider it analogous to the change in the bank account during the period. However, there are several items requiring explanation. Opportunity costs and the indirect effects of the investment on revenues and expenses of other products should be included (the effect on the bank account is indirect but real). Financial transactions affect the bank account but should not affect the cash flows. For example, payments of interest on debt require a cash disbursement but are not included in the computation of cash flow since the interest cost of the investment is taken into consideration via the discounting process. Depreciation expense is excluded because it does not affect the cash flow; however, the depreciation deducted for tax purposes does affect the tax bill and must be considered.[6] A fixed facility of a firm (for example, a boiler) may have excess capacity, and though using it does not re-

[6] The choice of the method of depreciation for tax purposes is itself a capital budgeting problem. The amounts of savings involved may be large.

quire cash outlay, it can be shown that there is merit in including a cost for such use in most situations.

Defining the "cash flow of period" is hard. But the main difficulty comes when we explicitly recognize that we can rarely know the future with certainty.

INVESTMENT DECISIONS AND UNCERTAINTY

How should one take risk into consideration? This is probably the most difficult of all tasks facing the decision maker. There is a temptation to vary the rate of discount, raising it for risky investments. This would move the decision in the correct direction (making it more difficult to accept the riskier investments), but it is an approximate method of taking risk into account and may easily give faulty results. There may be an investment for which practically all the risk is in the size of the outlays and little is in earning the revenues. For example, a public utility may be experimenting with an atomic power plant. Estimates of cost may range from $100 million to $500 million, and the plant may never operate at all. However, if the plant ever does operate, the utility may have a certain market for the electric power produced. Under these circumstances, applying a high rate of discount to the future revenues is not the correct method of taking the risky outlays into account.

The inability to adjust effectively for risk by varying the discount rate may be shown even more emphatically by this example: Assume we can make an investment of $400, and the two possible immediate outcomes are a payoff of $1,000 (with .5 probability) and a payoff of $0 (with .5 probability). The expected value of the payoffs is $500 and the outlay is $400; thus, there is net expected benefit of $100. However, there is risk (a .5 probability that there will be a loss of $400) so let us apply a high rate of time discount. But since the outcomes are immediate, it makes no difference what rate of discount we apply!

The effect of using different discount rates is difficult to anticipate. Assume that rates of discount of .10 and .20 are applied to two investments, each with a life of one year. Each dollar of cash flow of the less risky investment will be weighted 1.09 times more than a dollar of the risky investment. Now assume the return occurs in year 20; each dollar of the less risky investment will be weighted 5.69 times more than a dollar of the risky investment. It is difficult to see how the choice of a rate of discount would be made to take risk effectively into consideration.

In the above example, I computed the expected monetary value of the investment to be $100 where there is a $400 outlay and an immediate gamble involving two equally likely payoffs, one of $1,000 and one of $0. Despite the fact that the expected monetary value is positive, there are many persons who would reject the gamble as being too risky (I am among them). The outlay for the investment would have to be less than $100 before I would undertake the investment. This example (and there are other, more dramatic examples) illustrates a pitfall in the use of monetary expected value as a guide to action. Generally, in making investment analyses we assume either that the cash flows are known with certainty or that it is appropriate to use the mean, or expected value, of the cash flow of each period. If the investment outlay is small relative to the total wealth of the investor, the latter assumption is reasonable. However, if the outlays are large for the firm (or the component of the firm) making the decision, it may not be appropriate to be guided by expected monetary value. The extent of the dispersion of the possible outcomes may also be important, and equally so are the attitudes of the corporation or the decision maker toward the possible outcomes.

The literature of business and economics suggests the use of utility analysis and decision theory for decision-making under uncertainty. There have been systematic attempts to make a decision consistent with the preferences about risk of the party affected by the decision (in the context of the problem being discussed, this party is the corporation). This requires knowing the attitudes about risk as well as the probability distribution of the possible outcomes.

We can study the problem of investment decision-making under uncertainty on two levels. One level involves utility, probability, and statistical decision theory. These are complex tools beyond the scope of this discussion (though I can comment, without proof, that they are relevant and can contribute to improved decision-making).

The second level relies more on intuition. Once we recognize the facts that cash flows are not known with certainty and that the use of expected monetary value in a situation of uncertainty may not be valid if the sums involved are large in the view of the person (or organization) affected, then we are forced to move away from any one quantitative measure of profitability, be it a rate of return or present value. In the face of uncertainty, it may be desirable to look at an array of information about the investment — including the net present value computed at several rates of interest, since the proper rate of discount is itself uncertain, and different possible cash flows, since we do not know the flows with certainty. Some decision makers would also want to know the rate of return, the payback, and measures of the dispersion of the cash flows and of the net present values and how the cash flows of the investment are correlated with the present assets.

I have attempted to make clear that we can do several things reasonably well if we are not concerned with problems of uncertainty. We can make decisions to accept or reject independent investments and can choose the best of a set of mutually exclusive investments. Making these decisions requires an assumption that we can determine the appropriate discount rate. It is generally assumed that the cost of capital should be the cutoff rate in making these decisions.

However, the discussion of decision-making under conditions of uncertainty leads to the conclusion that it is incorrect to take risk into account by varying the rate of interest. This casts doubt on the correctness of using the cost of capital — which considers the attitudes of the stockholding community toward risk — as the general rate of discount. But if more risk is not handled by the use of a higher rate of interest, how is it to be handled? Here we have the problem of determining the utility function of a corporation or possibly even the utility function of the entire market (in the same manner that we may be interested in the rate of interest in the market and not the preferences about time value of an individual investor). The two prime unsolved conceptual problems in capital budgeting are the determination of the correct rate of discount and the incorporation of attitudes toward uncertainty in the analysis. Though the problems are not completely solved, there is much in the literature useful to a decision maker in business.

Business executives should seek to understand the investment decision. This may require tossing out any tried-and-true rules of thumb currently used, since the fact that the rules may have seemed to work is no proof that they are worthy of being carried into the future. A firm with a criterion of a two-year cutoff for payback is carrying a heavy anchor into the battle for world markets. Firms cutting off investments that promise returns of over 20 per cent because the additional investments would exceed the depreciation charge or the income of the year are using a criterion for decision that is difficult to defend. The economy needs additional investments by private corporations, and equally important, it needs investments made at the right time in the right place. There is no way of ensuring that this will be done perfectly, and there are sure to be incorrect investment decisions. But there are ways to improve the process of making investment decisions and to create procedures to make investment decisions that best serve the interests of both the stockholders and the economy.

Sources and Costs of Obtaining Funds

THE central focus of this paper is upon how management of the optimal financial mix can contribute to the profitability of a firm. "Financial mix" refers to the forms and sources of financing. It includes short- versus long-term financing, debt- versus equity-financing, various options that provide for mixed debt and equity forms, the relative use of internal and external financing as reflected in dividend policy, and the timing of the acquisition and disposition of funds. Also it includes analysis of comparative advantages in the use of alternative sources of funds — commercial banks, insurance companies, equity markets, and so forth.

Decisions about financing determine the cost-of-capital function for the firm. The cost of capital constitutes a cutoff point for accepting proposals for investment. Potential investment opportunities must offer profitability above some designated rate to be accepted in the capital budget of the firm to be financed.

Unfortunately, from the standpoint of offering practical guidance, considerable controversy rages with respect to the behavior of the cost of capital for individual firms. Fortunately, from the standpoint of enhancing understanding of the significance of financing, the disagreements have created an intellectual ferment, stimulating an analytical approach to the subject.

NOTE: This paper is a product of studies supported by a grant from the McKinsey Foundation for Management Research and aid from the Bureau of Business and Economic Research at the University of California at Los Angeles. The assistance of R. T. Aubey and A. S. Glazer is gratefully acknowledged.

THEORETICAL FRAMEWORK

Modigliani and Miller shook business finance theory from its traditional moorings with their now famous article [1] which argues that the value of a firm is determined by capitalizing its net operating income at an appropriate rate. Operations of arbitrage will prevent a leveraged firm from having a greater value than a less leveraged or unleveraged firm. This is their Proposition I.

The difference between Modigliani and Miller's theory and traditional business finance theory is indicated by Figures 1 and 2. In Figure 1, the Modigliani-Miller theory suggests that the cost of capital is con-

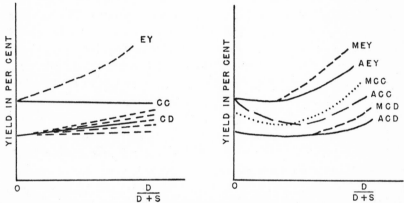

Figure 1. Model of costs of capital — Modigliani-Miller theory. EY represents yield on equity funds; CC, weighted cost of capital; CD, cost of debt; and $D/(D+S)$, leverage ratio at market values. *Figure 2.* Model of costs of capital — traditional business finance theory. MEY represents marginal equity yield; AEY, average equity yield; ACC, weighted cost of capital; MCC, weighted marginal cost of capital; MCD, marginal cost of debt; ACD, average cost of debt; and $D/(D+S)$, leverage ratio at market values.

[1] F. Modigliani and M. H. Miller, "The Cost of Capital, Corporation Finance and the Theory of Investment," *American Economic Review,* XLVIII (June 1958), 261–297; F. Modigliani and M. H. Miller, "Taxes and the Cost of Capital: A Correction," *American Economic Review,* LIII (June 1963), 433–443. See also Alexander Barges, *The Effect of Capital Structure on the Cost of Capital* (Englewood Cliffs, N.J.: Prentice-Hall, 1963); Gordon Donaldson, *Corporate Debt Capacity* (Boston: Harvard Business School, 1961); David Durand, "Costs of Debt and Equity Funds for Business: Trends and Problems of Measurement," *Conference on Research in Business Finance* (New York: National Bureau of Economic Research, 1952); Myron J. Gordon, "Security and a Financial Theory of Investment," *Quarterly Journal of Economics,* LXXIV (August 1960), 472–492; John Lintner, "The Cost of Capital and Optimal Financing of Corporate Growth," *Journal of Finance,* XVIII (May 1963), 292–310; Ezra Solomon, "Leverage and the Cost of Capital," *Journal of Finance,* XVIII (May 1963), 273–279.

stant for any range of leverage. The earnings-price ratio increases with leverage.[2] In their theory, the cost of debt will be such that the weighted cost of capital will be constant.

Traditional business finance theory, on the other hand, holds that for moderate amounts of leverage both the earnings-price ratio and the cost of debt rise little, if at all. As a consequence, the weighted cost of capital falls over an early range. At some point, established by financial traditions applicable to the individual industry, the earnings-price ratio on equity begins to rise with leverage. At a later point, the cost of debt begins to rise with leverage. In the range in which the earnings-price ratio begins to rise, two forces are working in opposite directions. The cost of equity rises, but the cost of debt is constant. With increased leverage, the debt of lower cost is weighted more heavily. Hence, there is likely to be a range, as in Figure 2, in which both the average and the marginal costs of capital are relatively constant. At some point, however, the earnings-price ratio begins to rise sharply, and the cost of debt also begins to rise, so that the curve for cost of capital turns upward.

In my view, traditional business finance provides a model which describes the behavior of business. First, one element in which both theories agree is that corporate income taxes provide an advantage to debt. Interest on debt is deductible as a cost for tax purposes, whereas dividends on preferred or common stock are not deductible.

Second, the risks of large corporations are not proportional to the risks of individuals. Large corporations represent a kind of insurance company for combining risks and thereby reducing the variance of expected return. Statistics of income amply support the contention that the variability of earnings among small firms is much greater than that for large corporations. As a consequence, the larger corporations represent a device for engaging in more leverage with less risk than could be achieved by individuals on their own account.

Third, as Ezra Solomon has pointed out, Modigliani and Miller appear to envisage a world in which equity costs reflect increased fi-

[2] The Modigliani-Miller diagram shows the earnings-price ratio as a linear function of leverage. However, in their formulation, leverage is defined as debt divided by stock (at market values). It can be shown that if the earnings-price ratio is a linear function of leverage, defined as debt over stock, it will be concave from above when expressed as a function of leverage defined as debt over debt plus stock. (Debt plus stock is defined as the total value of the firm.)

nancial risks owing to increased leverage, but debt costs do not rise with increased uncertainty.[3] This is contrary to the facts of life. But should the cost of debt rise with leverage, the costs-of-equity money would have to decline to hold the weighted cost of capital constant, as Modigliani and Miller aver. It is difficult to explain why investors should require rising risk premiums on equity yields as leverage increases, and then accept falling risk premiums beyond some degree of leverage.

Finally, the traditional business finance model for the real world is supported by a consideration of expectations. Economic theory states that under competitive conditions, if all factors of production correctly anticipate the future, each factor will receive its marginal-value product, and no one factor will obtain differential gains. In this sense one could generalize the Modigliani-Miller propositions: under full equilibrium conditions, no factor of production benefits from combinations of fixed and variable obligations or claims.

However, it is differences in expectations that lead to transactions in business and financial markets. An illustration of this generalization is the Alchian-Kessel theory with respect to the position of the firm as a net monetary debtor or creditor in relation to its expectations about future price levels.[4] The Alchian-Kessel thesis states that if price levels rise in the future, firms that are net-monetary debtors will gain, and firms that are net-monetary creditors will lose. The reverse will occur if price levels fall in the future. Traditional business finance theory generalizes the Alchian-Kessel thesis. It states that if debt holders (creditors) underestimate future earnings of the firm, on the average, equity owners will gain. Conversely, if equity holders as a group are overoptimistic as compared with debt holders, debt holders will gain because yields on debt will be higher and effective yields on equity lower than at equilibrium conditions.

This briefly sketches the major controversy between the Modigliani-Miller thesis and traditional business finance theory. I conclude that traditional business finance provides a better descriptive and normative theory of business financial policy than the Modigliani-Miller theory.

[3] Solomon, "Leverage and the Cost of Capital," pp. 277–278.
[4] R. A. Kessel, "Inflation-Caused Wealth Redistribution: A Test of a Hypothesis," *American Economic Review*, XLVI (March 1956), 218–241.

Profits in the Modern Economy

My replication of Modigliani and Miller's empirical tests supports traditional business finance as opposed to their assumptions.[5]

I now turn to a discussion of dividend policy. Again, Miller and Modigliani argue that dividend policy "does not matter." [6] They state that the value of the firm capitalizes the future stream of earnings — that it makes no difference whether this future stream of earnings results in all dividends, zero dividends, or a mix of dividends and retained earnings.

The essence of their argument is illustrated by the data in the certainty model on p. 140, based on their final equations. The data represent a certainty model with all equity financing.[7] The model shows that, regardless of dividend policy, total earnings will be the same. Total dividends, however, will depend upon the source of financing and will be greatest when all financing is external, lowest when all financing is internal.

Earnings per share start at the level of $10. The growth rate of earnings per share is greatest if all financing is internal and lowest if all financing is external, because then more shares will have to be sold to support the same rate of growth by a firm. If all financing is external,

[5] J. Fred Weston, "A Test of Cost of Capital Propositions," *Southern Economics Journal,* XXX (October 1963), 105–112.

[6] M. H. Miller and F. Modigliani, "Dividend Policy, Growth, and the Valuation of Shares," *Journal of Business,* XXXIV (October 1961), 411–433. See also Myron J. Gordon, "Dividends, Earnings, and Stock Prices," *Review of Economics and Statistics,* XLI (May 1959), 99–105, "The Savings Investment and Valuation of the Corporation," *Review of Economics and Statistics,* XLIV (February 1962), 37–51, and "Optimal Investment and Financing Policy," *Journal of Finance,* XVIII (May 1963), 264–272; John Lintner, "Distribution of Incomes of Corporations among Dividends, Retained Earnings and Taxes," *American Economic Review,* XLVI (May 1956), 97–113, and "Dividends, Earnings, Leverage, Stock Prices and the Supply of Capital to Corporations," *Review of Economics and Statistics,* XLIV (August 1962), 243–270; J. E. Walter, "Dividend Policies and Common Stock Prices," *Journal of Finance,* XI (March 1956), 29–41, and "Dividend Policy: Its Influence on the Value of the Enterprise," *Journal of Finance,* XVIII (May 1963), 280–291.

Professor Lintner's latest contribution to the analysis of financial policy introduced some practical assumptions. He has the internal profitability rate decline with an increased investment rate. The essence of his detailed analysis is equivalent to traditional marginal productivity theory. The traditional marginal productivity theory has been worked out in greatest detail for the labor input factor of production. In the Lintner analysis, it is worked out effectively for a marginal productivity theory of capital, particularly as it is influenced by equity financing mix decisions. See John Lintner, "Optimal Dividends and Corporate Growth under Uncertainty," *Quarterly Journal of Economics,* LXXVIII (February 1964), 49–95.

[7] Miller and Modigliani, "Dividend Policy," p. 423.

dividends per share will be the greatest, and if all financing is internal, dividends per share will be the lowest. Finally, the value of the firm is shown to be total initial earnings less the investment required to support the indicated rate of growth, to which is applied a multiplier of fifty.[8]

In a world of certainty and full equilibrium, the Miller-Modigliani dividend theory is correct. However, their model does not explain the real world, for the following reasons: First, just as the corporate income tax required modification of the Modigliani-Miller leverage model, so the personal income tax requires modification of the Miller-Modigliani dividend model. For the same rate of growth, a firm which financed from internal sources would avoid the personal income taxes paid by stockholders. Second, in a world of uncertainty and disequilibrium, differential opportunities are available to different firms. A firm with very favorable opportunities for making investments can utilize retained earnings more effectively than can stockholders by the alternatives available to them. As a consequence, firms with differentially higher profitability rates should have differentially higher growth rates and, therefore, will advantageously retain earnings rather than pay them out. Walter's model suggests that if the internal profitability rate of a firm is substantially greater than the market rate, the firm would retain earnings.[9] This is consistent with the practices of growth companies that in fact pay low or no dividends.

When carried to its logical conclusion, the Walter model suggests that dividend payouts be either zero or 100 per cent. But the model is consistent with the characteristic one-half to two-thirds dividend payouts observable in the real world. First, in a world of uncertainty, investors cannot expect individual firms to maintain internal profitability rates continuously above market rates. Hence, investors prefer to receive a portion of their earnings in hand, while permitting a portion of corporate earnings to remain in the corporate bush. Second, in a world of limited opportunities in the short run, whereas average profitability

---

[8] It will be noted that Miller and Modigliani have an all-equity-financing model. If we add debt, its influence would increase net earnings up to the critical degree of leverage and hence increase the value of the firm, because the multiplier would be increased only moderately. After the critical point of leverage is reached, it would be expected that the increment to net earnings would be offset by the increase in rho, the basic capitalization factor. As a consequence, the percentage to be divided into net earnings increases — the multiplier decreases.

[9] Walter, "Dividend Policies," pp. 29–41.

A Certainty Model of Dividend Policy, All Equity Financing

Measures of Results	1 All Internal Financing $k_e = 0, k_r = .4$	2 All External Financing $k_e = .4, k_r = 0$	3 Mixed Financing $k_e = .1, k_r = .3$
A. Total earnings	$\ln X(t) = \ln X(0) + k\rho^* t$ $\ln X(t) = \ln(\$1,000) + .08t$ $X(0) = \$2,159$	Same as A-1	Same as A-1
B. Total dividends	$\ln D(t) = \ln[X(0)(1 - k_r)] + k\rho^* t$ $= \ln(\$600) + .08t$ $D(10) = \$1,295$	$\ln D(t) = \ln[X(0)(1 - k_r)] + k\rho^* t$ $= \ln(\$1,000) + .08t$ $D(10) = \$2,159$	$\ln D(t) = \ln[X(0)(1 - k_r)] + k\rho^* t$ $= \ln(\$700) + .08t$ $D(10) = \$1,511$
C. Earnings per share	$\ln x(t) = \ln x(0) + gt$ $g = k\rho^*$ $\ln x(t) = \ln(\$10) + .08t$ $x(10) = \$21.59$	$\ln x(t) = \ln x(0) + gt$ $g = \dfrac{k(\rho^* - \rho)}{1 - k}$ $\ln x(t) = \ln(\$10) + .067t$ $x(10) = \$19.13$	$\ln x(t) = \ln x(0) + gt$ $g = k\rho^*\left(\dfrac{1 - k_r}{1 - k}\right) - k_e\rho\left(\dfrac{1}{1 - k}\right)$ $\ln x(t) = \ln(\$10) + .076t$ $x(10) = \$20.80$
D. Dividends per share	$\ln d(t) = \ln[x(0)(1 - k_r)] + gt$ $g = k\rho^*$ $\ln d(t) = \ln(\$6) + .08t$ $d(10) = \$12.95$	$\ln d(t) = \ln[x(0)(1 - k_r)] + gt$ $g = $ same as g in C-2 $\ln d(t) = \ln(\$10) + .067t$ $d(10) = \$19.13$	$\ln d(t) = \ln[x(0)(1 - k_r)] + gt$ $g = $ same as g in C-3 $\ln d(t) = \ln(\$7) + .076t$ $d(10) = \$14.56$
E. Value of firm	$V(0) = \dfrac{X(0)(1 - k)}{\rho - \rho^* k}$ $= \dfrac{\$600}{.10 - .08} = \dfrac{\$600}{.02}$ $= \$30,000$	Same as E-1	Same as E-1

SOURCE: Adapted from M. H. Miller and F. Modigliani, "Dividend Policy, Growth, and the Valuation of Shares," *Journal of Business*, XXXIV (October 1961), 423, published by the University of Chicago Press, copyright 1961 by the University of Chicago.

Key, with some illustrative values

$X(0) = $ total initial earnings of the firm $= \$1,000$
$D(0) = $ total initial dividends of the firm
$N = $ total initial number of shares of common stock $= 100$
$x(0) = $ initial earnings per share $= \$10$
$d(0) = $ initial dividends per share
$\rho = $ market rate of return $= 10\%$

$\rho^* = $ internal rate of return $= 20\%$
$t = $ time
$k = $ ratio of investment to total earnings in time $(t) = .4$
$k_e = $ investment financed from external sources
$k_r = $ investment financed from internal sources

140

rates are above the market rate for individual firms in a given time period, the marginal profit rates on available opportunities fall to market rates before all internal funds are exhausted.

This paper has thus far sought to establish that in a world of uncertainty and disequilibrium both debt and dividend policy appear capable of influencing the value of the enterprise. Other problems in the analysis of the cost of capital may now be examined.

SOME MEASUREMENT PROBLEMS IN CALCULATING COST OF CAPITAL

Many of the additional issues associated with cost-of-capital analysis of financing mix are related to procedures of measurement. This section will cover a number of important issues.

Coupon Rates versus Opportunity Costs. The choice between coupon rates or some other cost for debt can be settled quickly. Clearly, the relevant consideration is the opportunity cost of funds. The opportunity cost of funds to a particular firm depends on its risk class and other sets of circumstances. Also, it is clear from the foregoing that the cost of capital cannot be discussed independently of the level of opportunities available to the firm.

The question of the reinvestment rate may now be considered: In a world of uncertainty and partial disequilibrium, the dynamics of the economy give rise to above-normal opportunities for profit. For some firms, the internal average rate of profitability for the firm will be greater than the market rate. The firm is operating in an imperfect market in the sense described by Schumpeter as necessary to induce investment for innovation.

Consequently, the value of the marginal product lies above the marginal value product, the situation depicted in Figure 3. In Figure 3, the value of the marginal product is above the marginal value of product — the marginal efficiency investment curve for the firm. The firm will, therefore, raise funds to the point where the marginal value product curve intersects the marginal cost-of-capital function. Thus the opportunity cost is not the average reinvestment profit of the firm, but rather the marginal cost of capital. Hence the reinvestment problem has been handled satisfactorily.

Current Yield versus Growth Yield. The next problem to be considered is the question of the use of the current dividend or earnings-price ratio versus the growth yield (future earnings or dividends to current price over the relevant time horizon) as the cost of equity money.[10] For companies with no growth in expected earnings, no problem is posed because the current yield is the same as the growth yield. Companies with expected growth in earnings and/or dividends are likely to sell on a basis of current yield lower than its growth yield. Clearly, companies could not sell on a basis of a yield of 2 per cent, or fifty times

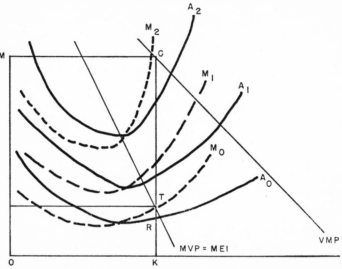

Figure 3. Excess of value of the marginal product of capital over the weighted average and marginal cost of capital. VMP represents value of the marginal product of capital; MVP, marginal value product of capital; MEI, marginal efficiency of capital; A_0, weighted average cost of capital for optimal leverage; A_1, weighted average cost of capital for small leverage; A_2, weighted average cost of capital for excessive leverage; M_0, weighted marginal cost of capital for optimal leverage; M_1, weighted marginal cost of capital for small leverage; and M_2, weighted marginal cost of capital for excessive leverage.

earnings, unless future growth was expected. It is the promise of higher earnings in the future that results in a higher price in the present.

The point may be illustrated by the analogy of a merger. In a merger, one company may be valued at a price-earnings ratio of thirty; another firm may be valued at a price-earnings ratio of ten. This difference reflects the expectation of higher earnings on the part of the firm with the price-earnings ratio of thirty, or its greater contribution to combined

[10] R. M. Soldofsky and J. T. Murphy, *Growth Yields on Common Stock — Theory and Tables* (Iowa City: State University of Iowa, 1963).

earnings in the merged firm. But without true merger-economies, the companies are merely trading gains and losses.[11] In a like manner, the investor would not pay fifty times earnings for a stock when he can obtain higher current yields on other investments, unless he expected the profit rates to be differentially higher than for other investments.[12]

A company whose common stock is selling on a low current-yield basis can obtain money on a current basis on favorable terms. But a high rate of growth of earnings must be achieved to validate the high current price. To have sold the stock on a low current-yield basis is an advantage. In a price-and-profit, enterprise economy, differentially higher rates of growth and profitability are likely to attract a flow of resources. As a consequence, it is difficult for any company to achieve differentially higher profits and differentially higher growth rates in profits over a sustained period of time. (Notable exceptions, such as IBM, only prove the rule.)

During periods of optimism, the future amount and duration of differential profitability and growth for a firm are likely to be overoptimistically evaluated by equity investors. Furthermore, equity investors will probably be influenced greatly by performance in recent years and tend to extrapolate it. Hence, in a company in which earnings have recently been growing at a high rate, profitability may be overvalued, at least part of the time. The price of the stock of the firm may be expected to be subject to much greater swings of optimism and pessimism.[13]

This, then, is the advantage of being able to sell equity money on a basis of low current yield. If the expectations of higher profitability rates and higher growth rates of profitability are not achieved, the company has sold its equity on a relatively more favorable basis than would have been possible otherwise. This represents a special case of the more general situation described above. Financial policies such as those concerning leverage and dividends represent taking positions with regard to the future. Whereas neither the firm nor the investors could gain under positions of certainty and equilibrium, the long run is, in the real

[11] D. F. Folz and J. Fred Weston, "Looking Ahead in Evaluating Proposed Mergers," *National Accounting Association Bulletin*, April 1962, pp. 17–27.

[12] C. C. Holt, "The Influence of Growth Duration on Share Prices," *Journal of Finance*, XVII (September 1962), 465–475; B. G. Malkiel, "Equity Yields and Structure of Share Prices," *American Economic Review*, LIII (December 1963), 1004–1031.

[13] See in this connection B. G. Malkiel, "Equity Yields."

world, a series of short runs characterized by uncertainty and disequilibrium. If investors in either equities or debt are overoptimistic or overpessimistic, the financial managers of the enterprise acquiring funds may achieve gains by altering the financial mix. In theory, no net gains are achieved. In a world of change and uncertainty, expectations must err on both sides. It is differences in expectations that make markets and lead to specialization of functions and selection of positions as debtor or creditor in obtaining and supplying funds.

Companies selling on the basis of a current yield of 2 per cent may in fact have an equity cost of 8 to 10 per cent. How can this be de-

Table 1. Pattern of Growth Yields

Firms in Different Industries	Cost of Capital	Return-on-Capital Target	Expansion Profit Goal
Electric utility	...	6½–7%	...
Telephone	...	8%	...
Department stores	8%	At least above bare cost	up to 20%
Industrial company, average	10%	At least above bare cost	up to 20%
Textile	13%	At least above bare cost	up to 20%

SOURCE: John F. Childs, "Profit Goals for Management," *Financial Executive*, XXXII (February 1964), 20.

termined? In theory, we must have an estimate of the future growth rate in earnings over the appropriate time horizon or over a series of time horizons. By relating this series of future earnings to current price, we can develop a growth yield that measures the relation between the future stream of earnings and the present price.[14] John F. Childs suggests the pattern set forth in Table 1.[15] Childs's data suggest a range from 6½ to 13 per cent as the over-all cost of capital. Since the cost of debt money is usually less than the growth-yield cost of equity money, the weighted average figures provided by Childs suggest a higher cost of equity than of all capital for the spread of industries represented.

[14] Soldofsky and Murphy, *Growth Yields*.
[15] John F. Childs, "Profit Goals for Management," *Financial Executive*, XXXII (February 1964), 13–23.

The reason for the difference in the cost of equity money for firms in different industries lies primarily in the presence of risk or uncertainty associated with investment for different lines of activity. This, in turn, leads to an analysis of the role of uncertainty.

Treatment of Uncertainty. A number of difficulties exist in handling the factor of uncertainty since, by definition, uncertainty relates to the unknown and unknowable. The scope of this paper certainly does not permit a detailed treatment of the problem of uncertainty. However, the major implications may be suggested.

Because of the existence of uncertainty, we cannot talk about maximizing a single profit figure. Rather, there are probability distributions associated with expected returns. What are the bases for the probability distributions? One is characteristic experience in the line of business — i.e., the probability distributions may have a basis in relative frequency. On the other hand, lack of adequate data may require the use of Bayesian subjective probability estimates.[16]

A more uncertain future return will have a probability distribution with a wider range of possible returns. The degree of uncertainty may be measured by the second, third, or fourth moments of the probability distribution. The second moment is variance, the third a measure of skewness, and the fourth a measure of kurtosis.[17] When the variance of the probability distribution is taken as a measure of uncertainty, the discount factor applied to the expected returns, or the range of expected returns, is a positive function of the degree of uncertainty.

We do not have equations relating the risk premium to the kinds of factors that determine it.[18] However, we need only to understand the nature and direction of the relation. Given the nature of uncertainty, we must depend upon market forces to move uncertainty and risk premiums to their partial and temporary equilibrium levels in the process of working toward full equilibrium.

[16] R. Schlaifer, *Probability and Statistics for Business Decisions* (New York: McGraw-Hill, 1959).

[17] Alexander M. Mood and Franklin A. Graybill, *Introduction to the Theory of Statistics* (New York: McGraw-Hill, 1963), pp. 107–117.

[18] But a start has been made — see Lawrence Fisher, "Determinants of Risk Premiums on Corporate Bonds," *Journal of Political Economy*, LXVII, No. 3 (June 1959), 217–237; Haskell Benishay, "Variability in Earnings-Price Ratios of Corporate Equities," *American Economic Review*, LI (March 1961), 81–94; D. Meiselman, *The Term Structure of Interest Rates* (Englewood Cliffs, N.J.: Prentice-Hall, 1962).

Profits in the Modern Economy

In general terms, it may be said that in the face of uncertainty two major classes of devices are employed by decision makers. One is portfolio theory.[19] The decision maker analyzes various combinations of expected returns, variances, and covariances. Through programing of individual investment opportunities involving different combinations of expected returns, variances, and covariances, efficient portfolio sets can be identified. Efficient portfolios minimize variance for target return; or for a maximum acceptable variance, they achieve a maximum expected return. Portfolio theory provides a mechanism for efficiently combining groups of independent investment opportunities. The selection among efficient portfolios depends upon the preferences of the decision maker. In the absence of institutional constraints (such as legal lists) or traditions of conservatism among various kinds of investors, market forces will result in patterns of equilibrium of diverse premiums for different situations of uncertainty.

The other major device for dealing with uncertainty is the adoption of various kinds of strategies. The first example is that of using more flexible methods of production in the face of possible fluctuations in demand.[20] A relatively higher ratio of variable to fixed costs is applied in the face of uncertainty, as well as a relatively smaller proportion of special machinery and fixed equipment. In the realm of financial policy, opportunities for recontracting (such as options to call) or for exercising options in the form of convertibles and warrants will be taken. Positions may be hedged through the use of recontracting devices, options, and various long- or short-term positions with regard to the net monetary status of the corporation as debtor or creditor.

The foregoing has analyzed the essential problems related to the determination of the cost of capital of business firms that center on the significant theoretical issues. The theoretical issues dealt with have been debt policy; dividend policy; the choice of reinvestment rate; the use of current versus growth yields; the treatment of uncertainty, broken

---

[19] H. Markowitz, "Portfolio Selection," *Journal of Finance*, VII (March 1952), 77–91, and *Portfolio Selection: Efficient Diversification of Investments* (New York: Wiley, 1960); H. A. Latane, "Criteria for Choice among Risky Ventures," *Journal of Political Economy*, LXVII (April 1959), 144–155; D. E. Farrar, *The Investment Decision under Uncertainty* (Englewood Cliffs, N.J.: Prentice-Hall, 1962); H. M. Weingartner, *Mathematical Programming and the Analysis of Capital Budgeting Problems* (Englewood Cliffs, N.J.: Prentice-Hall, 1963).

[20] G. H. Stigler, "Production and Distribution in the Short Run," in *Journal of Political Economy*, XLVII (1939), 305–327.

down between probability distributions of different ranges and appropriate discount factors associated with different moments of probability distributions; the use of portfolio theory; and the adoption of broad strategies in dealing with the problem of uncertainty.

I now turn to the practical implementation of the concepts discussed above. The theoretical framework suggests that the following variables should be considered relevant for analyzing the cost of the financing mix for business firms: industry or risk class; profitability rate; rate of growth of sales and profits; instability of sales and profits; age, size, and stage in life cycle of the industry and firm; leverage; changes in price level; economic environmental factors; and term, structure, and form of claims.

The cost of capital for business firms is a function of these many variables. To determine the influence of any one variable on the cost of capital of a firm, we would, in theory, take a partial derivative of the equation with respect to the factor we are permitting to vary, holding all the others constant.[21] Rather than attempt such a formal approach, it would appear more useful for purposes of this study to analyze the cost of capital for firms by qualitative judgments of the influence of each of these variables.

Nature of the Major Influences — General. The list above may be grouped into three kinds of variables. The first set relates to the broad economic environment, including expected growth rates and possible instabilities of the economy. It allows for expected fluctuations of price levels, as well as shifts in relative factor costs. It also encompasses considerations about balance of payments, which in turn reflect relative factor costs and relative rates and patterns of growth and development in the individual economies of the world.

The second set of factors concerns the characteristics of individual industries and includes five variables. These are the rate of growth of sales and profits in the industry, the instability of sales and profits in the industry, age, size, and stage of life cycle of the industry and firm. Each has a significant influence on the opportunities available to a firm and on the kinds of investment and financial activities in which it engages.

[21] See the equations in Myron J. Gordon, *The Investment Financing and Valuation of the Corporation* (Homewood, Ill.: Irwin, 1962).

The third set of factors deals with the pattern of investments of the particular firm and its pattern of financing mix. Decisions about this set will determine the over-all structure of the firm's position — whether it is long or short with regard to present and future fluctuations in prices, relative factor costs, and relative profitability or opportunities.

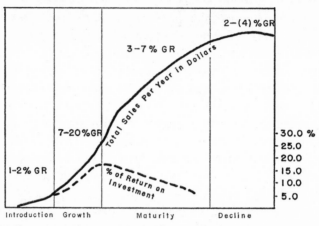

Figure 4. Illustrative life cycle of product or industry. Percentage of growth rate per annum of dollars of sales (GR) represented by solid line; profit margins measured by percentage of return on investment represented by broken line (right scale).

The Financial Life Cycle of the Firm. To illustrate these general concepts, I shall outline the life cycle of financing characteristics and costs of an individual firm. First, consider the life cycle of an industry — the nature of which can be summarized. Figure 4 outlines the conceptual scheme, in which four stages may be identified: introduction, growth, maturity, and decline.

Many economic characteristics associated with the life cycle might be considered; this paper will focus on growth rates and profit margins. In the stage of introduction, growth rates are relatively low. However, as the product achieves acceptance and a reservoir of demand is being satisfied, growth rates are high, ranging from 7 to 20 per cent. It is at this point in the life cycle of the industry that growth firms predominate and profit margins are at their peak.

In the stage of maturity, growth levels off to rates characteristic of the particular line of business. In the food industry, for example, the growth rate is likely to be dominated by the growth rate of the population. If the product is a luxury, the growth rate is likely to be dominated by the growth rate in the number of family units with incomes above a certain level, such as $8,000. The high profit margins of the growth stage of the industry have attracted more resources so that sales-to-capacity relations are likely to be less favorable in the maturity phase of the industry. Consequently, profit margins decline. Finally, the rise of substitute products leads to the fourth stage, a decline in the growth rate of the industry. Profit margins will be further narrowed and may even become negative.

The concept of the life cycle is not offered as a rigorous theory, but as a useful conceptual framework for discussing some changes in the life cycle of industries and firms that have important implications for financial policy. I postulate the origination of a new firm, distinguishing between a new, small firm in an old industry and a new firm in a new industry. The industries in which the new, small firms predominate are mainly those in retail and wholesale trade and are relatively mature. High mortality rates of firms reflect a tendency toward overcapacity and too many firms in industries in retail and wholesale trade. New, small firms in retail and wholesale trade can hope to command neither tremendous enthusiasm for their prospects nor unusually favorable opportunities. Therefore, such new, small firms must depend initially on the funds of the owners and their friends and relatives,[22] supplemented by credit from trade suppliers who, in turn, are anxious to develop new outlets for their products.

Financing is somewhat easier for new firms in new industries with high profit opportunities, although risks are still great because mortality rates for new firms are likewise high. It is often difficult to identify in advance the probabilities of success or failure, and as a consequence, financing sources in the initial stages may also be limited. Established sources, such as commercial banks and insurance companies, cannot undertake the risks for the limited uncertain returns promised. The established equity and bond markets will not accept the securities of firms whose records of earnings and performance have not been established.

[22] Victor Andrews, Seymour Friedland, and Eli Shapiro, "Working-Capital Financing of Small Business," *Law and Contemporary Problems*, XXIV (Winter 1959), 68–88; Federal Reserve System, *Financing Small Business*, A Report to the Committees on Banking and Currency and the Select Committees on Small Business, United States Congress (Washington, D.C.: United States Government Printing Office, 1958).

Profits in the Modern Economy

Investment development companies find that they must look at a tremendously large number of new firms before they find some that appear to be attractive for possible financing.[23] As a general matter, therefore, the bulk of initial financing must come from the owners, their friends and relatives.

If the small firm prospers and grows, the owners will seek to finance from internal sources and by external debt. They will use trade credit and other forms of debt in the effort to avoid selling common stock to outsiders. However, at some point established standards of debt-to-equity ratios for the industry require that additional equity be sold. This typically will occur in the rapid growth segment in the life cycle of growth of the firm. Since the sales and profits of the firm are still growing, some form of option is likely to be employed in an attempt to sell equities at a future price.

Additional financing may be required in the third stage of the growth cycle. If so, debt will be employed until established leverage standards are reached, and then straight equity will be employed. As the firm moves into the third stage of its life cycle, its growth rate slows. The third stage of the life cycle of the growth of firms is likely to be the stage of longest duration. At this point the firm has matured; it becomes an established enterprise.

It is characteristic of firms of stable size in the mature phase of the life cycle of the industry and firm that they employ relatively little debt. In fact, during the third stage the firm may pay off the debt incurred in the second stage. Often, firms do not continue to employ debt to increase returns to net worth because of the desire to avoid the risks of debt. With a slower growth and at least moderate profitability rates, internal sources of funds may be adequate to meet the new investment requirements of the firm. Thus the cycle of financing is completed.

CONTRIBUTIONS OF FINANCIAL POLICY TO PROFITABILITY

The numerous theoretical and environmental threads may now be brought together. The central question is, How can financial policies and decisions contribute to an increase in the profitability of firms? The answer must be related to the basic characteristics of both forms and sources of financing.

[23] Gordon Baty, *Initial Financing of the New Research-Based Enterprise in New England*, Research Report to Federal Reserve Bank of Boston, No. 25, 1964.

Forms of Financing. Table 2 suggests important characteristics of forms of funds. It focuses on differences in the fixity of obligations and on the effects of choice of form on control of the enterprise; it comments on the flexibility of the form of financing; and finally, it indicates the tax deductibility of the cost of each form of financing.

In general, short-term, unsecured forms of financing involve the least loss of control because the lender of funds can review his commitment at short intervals. All secured forms of short-, intermediate-,

Table 2. Characteristics of Forms of Funds

Forms of Funds	Fixed Cost	Fixed Maturity Date	Tax Deduct- ible	Loss of Control	Flexibility
Long-Term Financing					
Common stock	Limited to dividends	No	No	Yes, if new share- holders	Widens financial base
Preferred stock	Limited to dividends	No	No	Some	Some restrictions
Debt-bonds	Yes	Yes	Yes	Indenture provisions	Bond restrictions
Retained earnings	No	Avoids double taxation	No	No	No restrictions
Intermediate Financing					
Conditional sales contract	Interest	Yes	Yes	Some	Must meet payments
Leasing	Yes	Yes	Yes	Some	Must meet payments
Short-Term-Unsecured Financing					
Trade credit	No	Discount date and due date	Yes	Some	Frees cash
Commercial banks	Interest	Yes	Yes	Some restrictions	Restricts
Commercial paper	Interest	Yes	Yes	No	No effect
Short-Term-Secured Financing					
Accounts receivable financing	No	Yes	Yes	Some	Sales generate funds
Accounts receivable factoring	No	Yes	Yes	Some	Restrict buyers
Inventory financing	No	Yes	Yes	Some	Inventory controls

Table 3. Summary of Characteristics of Alternative Sources of Financing

Source of Funds	Duration of Use of Funds	Form of Financing Supplies	Degree of Risk Taken by Source of Funds	Stability of Availability of Funds	Facilities for Mass Financing	Nature of Contact	Amount of Management Counsel
Commercial banks	Mainly short term, some medium	Debt	High quality	Cyclical variations	Limited	Close	Moderate to considerable
Life insurance companies	Medium to long term	Mostly debt	High quality	Secular growth	Limited	Limited but direct	Small to moderate
Finance companies	Continuing	Debt	Considerable	Cyclical	Considerable	Close	Small to considerable
Mutual savings banks	Long term	Debt	Secured by real estate	Stable	None	Indirect	None
Fire and casualty insurance companies	Long term	Debt and equity	Moderate	Variable	None	Indirect	Small
Investment companies	Long term	Debt and equity	High quality	Variable	None	Indirect	None

	Term	Type	Quality	Stability		Relationship	Amount
Pension funds	Long term	Debt and equity	High quality	Stable	None	Indirect	None
Savings and loan associations	Long term	Debt	Medium to low	Stable	None	Direct	None
Educational and religious funds	Long term	Debt and equity	High quality	Variable	None	Indirect	None
Investment development	Long term	Debt and equity	Moderate to high	Stable	None	Direct and close	Considerable
Development credit corporations	Long term	Debt	Moderate to high	Stable	None	Direct and close	Small to large
Federal lending and loan insurance	Short, medium, and long	Debt	Low to moderate	Erratic	None	Direct	Small to large
Employees	Long term	Mostly equity	Moderate to high	Erratic	None	Direct	None
Customers	Long term	Debt and equity	Moderate to high	Erratic	None	Indirect	None
Equity markets	Permanent	Equity	Full range	Erratic	None	Indirect	None
Interbusiness suppliers	Short, medium, and long	Debt and equity	Continuing low to high	Variable	Small	Close and direct	Small to considerable

and long-term debt have the advantage of tying the amount of financing to the levels of assets that generate both the need for funds and the security for obtaining loans. However, a gap between the size of the security and the amount of the loan remains; thus, all forms of debt require some equity base.

Debt forms of financing are generally less costly than equity forms if the growth yield of equity funds is taken into account. The two reasons for choosing equity forms are (1) such funds are necessary to provide a base for the use of debt, and (2) there are times when advantages of equity financing offset the lower cost of debt financing.

The basic characteristics of sources of financing (set forth in Table 3) focus on the degree of risk accepted by the source of funds, the duration of the use of funds, the nature of contacts, and the amount of managerial counsel that may be provided. A wide range of sources with a complex spectrum of qualities is offered because any one source possesses both advantages and disadvantages. The needs of the firm at a particular time must be related to the special characteristics of the source of financing.

Sources of financing tend to specialize in particular forms by virtue of the nature of their own funds. Partly owing to characteristics of its funds and partly to the nature of its experience, an individual source of funds attempts to obtain a relative advantage in particular segments of financial markets.

The cost of funds is not discussed in Table 3 because cost is more a function of the circumstances of the firm and of the general economic environmental conditions. Also, it is useful and important to emphasize that the availability of funds may be more important to firms than their absolute cost. The profitability opportunities may be so favorable as to make it advantageous to employ funds at very high costs. In this connection, individual firms can increase the availability of funds to them by a number of managerial devices — one method is keeping systematic records of past events, another is careful study of the future as expressed in plans and budgets. Such keeping of records and making of budgets by firms seeking funds can aid potential sources of funds appraise the probable future of the enterprises. Better analysis, control, and planning reduce the subjective and actual risks to the sources of funds; thus the availability of funds is increased as sources react to the lesser risk.

I now turn to the factors that may influence the relative cost of funds from alternative forms of financing. Figure 5 indicates the time trend of the costs of selected sources of funds since 1950 at different stages of the business cycle. On a basis of the time trend since 1950, the cost of equity funds, when measured on a basis of current yield, has decreased, whereas the cost of debt funds has increased. Unfortunately, regularly published data on growth yields of equity are not available. The

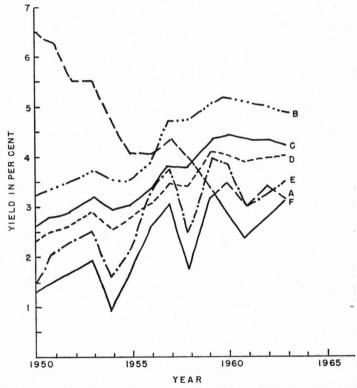

Figure 5. Variability of costs of financing over time. Line A represents common stock dividend yields; B, corporation bonds, Baa quality; C, corporation bonds, Aaa quality; D, United States taxable bonds; E, commercial paper, four to six months; and F, three-month United States treasury bills. (From *Economic Report of the President*, 1964, pp. 265, 288.)

costs of debt funds characteristically decline during cyclical downturns in general business. The spread in the cost of debt of different maturities has fluctuated with varying economic environmental conditions. The data demonstrate a noticeable widening in the spread between the costs of different debt forms of financing during recession years.

Figure 6 presents impressionistically the term structure of the cost of different forms of financing for different years since 1950. The data indicate a decline in the spread between the costs of financing at different maturities in recent years. This culminates in operation twist in 1961–1964, when the spread between the cost of short- and of long-term funds was narrowed.

Figures 5 and 6 suggest that changed environmental conditions make for significant variations in the cost of alternative forms of financing. These environmental conditions may be joined with characteristics of industry and firm that together provide a wide range of possible variations. The opportunities may be combined to achieve a financing mix that will contribute to enterprise profitability. The nature of these variables is suggested by Table 4, elements of which will not be examined

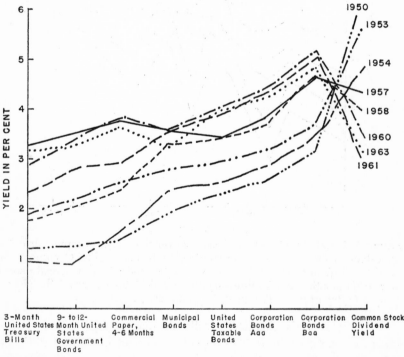

Figure 6. Term structure of financing costs for selected years between 1950 and 1963. (From *Economic Report of the President,* 1964, pp. 265, 288.)

in detail. Suffice it to focus on the significant variations in factors influencing the cost of financing: these may be related to the level of economic activity, in turn influenced by monetary and fiscal policies as well as the position of the nation regarding the international balance of payments.

With regard to industries, three classes of characteristics are identified: The first is the durability of goods. In general, the industries producing durable goods are subject to wide fluctuations in sales and profits. The second is competitive structure. The extent to which an industry is characterized by oligopoly is influenced by the degree to which heavy fixed costs may be required for entry into the industry; the prevalence of monopolistic competition is influenced by possibilities of product differentiation. The third is the stage in the life cycle of the industry. Significant variations occur in the rate of growth of sales and of profit margins at different stages in the life cycle of an industry, and these are related in turn to the corresponding costs of equity and debt, balanced against other economic characteristics of the environment.

Finally, the characteristics of firms are analyzed — the important ones are product mix, absolute size, the firm's share of the market, stage in the life cycle of its growth, and age. The characteristic that stands out is high variability and changes in the relations of the underlying variables.

The large number of variables affecting forms and sources of financing reflect the life cycle of the industries and firms and the changes in general economic environmental conditions. Costs of different forms and sources of financing change in relation to a large number of influences. These factors are related to conditions of disequilibrium in the economy that produce abundant opportunities for substantial contributions to profitability by good financial management.

Clearly, an individual firm is likely at different times during its life cycle to employ most of the forms and sources of financing outlined, and it is certain to use some simultaneously at different stages of its development. The appropriate mix varies with changes in general environmental conditions as well as with changes in the characteristics of the industry and firm. I conclude, therefore, that good financial management can potentially contribute substantially to profitability of the enterprise.

Table 4. Variables Influencing Costs of Financing

Variable		Effect on		
	Sales	Profit Margins	Cost of Equity	Cost of Debt
Environmental				
Stage of economic conditions				
Expansion	Increasing	Rising	Decreasing	Rising
Peak of expansion	Peak	Leveling	Beginning to rise	Near peak
Contraction	Decreasing	Falling	Increasing	Decreasing
Trough of contraction	Low	Beginning to rise	Beginning to fall	Near bottom
Monetary policy				
Increasing money supply	Increasing	Increasing	Decreasing	Decreasing
Decreasing money supply	Decreasing	Decreasing	Increasing	Increasing
Fiscal policy				
Surplus	Decrease	Decrease	Decrease	Decrease
Deficit	Increase	Increase	Increase	Increase
Balance of payments				
Surplus	Increase	Increase	Decrease	Decrease
Deficit	Decrease	Decrease	Increase	Increase

Industry

Competitive structure				
Oligopolistic	Stable	Stable	Low	Low
Highly competitive	Volatile	Volatile	High	High
Type of good produced				
Durable	Volatile	Volatile	High	High
Nondurable	Stable	Stable	Low	Low
Stage in life cycle				
Beginning	Volatile	Low	High	High
Growth	Growing	High	Medium–Low	Medium–Low
Maturity	Stable	Moderate	Low	Low
Decline	Declining	Low	High–Medium	High–Medium

Firm

Product mix				
Balanced	Stable	Stable	Low–Medium	Low
Dependent on one or a few similar products	Volatile	Volatile	High–Medium	Medium
Size-absolute				
Large	Variable	Variable	Low	Low
Small	Variable	Variable	High–Medium	High
Size-share of market				
Large	Stable	Stable	Low	Low
Small	Variable	Variable	High–Medium	High–Medium
Stage in life cycle				
Introduction	Volatile	Low–Moderate	High	High
Growth	Rapid Growth	Low	Low	Low
Maturity	Moderate Growth	Moderate	Moderate	Low
Decline	Declining	Low	High–Medium	High–Medium

Age

Young (0–5 yrs)	Variable	Variable	High	High
5–10 yrs	Variable	Variable	Moderate–Low	Moderate
Long established	Variable	Variable	Low	Low

ROBERT K. JAEDICKE

THE process of capital budgeting can be briefly outlined as follows: (1) for investment projects, determine the relevant cash flows after income taxes; (2) choose a criterion or criteria by which projects will be selected or rejected; and (3) determine the sources of capital to be used in financing the capital budget. Obviously, these steps are not mutually exclusive, nor are they necessarily in order. That is, the financing problem and the choice of certain criteria for investment selection are certainly related, as Weston has so adequately demonstrated. However, in the determination of its program of capital investment, any firm must engage in these three steps — the relative importance and complexity of each will vary from firm to firm and perhaps from investment project to investment project.

As both Bierman and Weston have noted, this over-all process is carried out under conditions of uncertainty. This poses a difficult problem for students and practitioners of capital budgeting; much research still needs to be done. These two papers provide a good discussion of the over-all process of capital budgeting as I have outlined it above. They have discussed many of the problems but also have pointed out some things that we can already do quite adequately. I shall confine my comments to some of the important problems of capital budgeting which were not covered in detail. Since I am an accountant, I shall discuss these papers and capital budgeting generally from an accountant's point of view, leaving to Messrs. Johnson and Holland the job of discussing the papers from the financier's point of view.

DISCOVERING PROPOSALS FOR CAPITAL INVESTMENT

In order to do a good job of selecting capital-investment projects, one must first know about them. Yet this is a part of the process of capital budgeting which has received little attention. In a real sense, the best and most refined methods of determining cash flows and cost of capital are of little value to a manager if he cannot first be fairly certain that he knows about the possible investment opportunities that exist within the firm. If such an informational system does not exist, we may do an excellent job of selecting projects inferior to ones which were never considered.

It is frequently suggested that the capital-budgeting decision is one which should not be decentralized, and it is true that decentralization in this area presents some important problems. But all the good methodology in the world won't help if headquarters doesn't know of good opportunities. Perhaps what is needed here is a full-scale, rigorous educational campaign that will carry to managers at all levels the capital-investment story. It doesn't make much difference whether the manager-students actually make decisions about capital investment. Capital budgeting is a highly interesting and intriguing subject; education in its problems at all levels of management should do much to prevent potentially profitable projects from lying fallow because of non-discovery.

MONITORING INVESTMENT PROJECTS

Another problem we frequently overlook in our continual search for improved methodology is what to do about following up on projects once they have been accepted. Many descriptions of the process of capital investment read as if it were just a matter of selecting or rejecting investments. What happens when we do accept a new building, or even a new machine? After the decision our problems are usually just beginning — that is, the period of installation and complete debugging of the new process may be long and filled with difficulties. Some follow-up or postaudit procedures need to be established to aid the manager in determining when the project is going well so that he and his staff can turn to the next project.

In this regard, we often overlook the constraint imposed by the shortage of technicians required to install and fully integrate capital investments. Early in 1950 a capital investment study called *The Minneapolis Project* was conducted at the University of Minnesota by a group headed by Arthur Upgren and including Francis Boddy, Carl Nelson, and Walter Heller. (This pilot study was published on July 21, 1950, by the School of Business Administration of the University of Minnesota, marking the completion of a study undertaken at the invitation of Investors Diversified Services.) The study showed that the shortage of (or limitations on) technically trained people required to carry out investment projects was in many cases as serious a constraint as the limited supply of capital. I suspect that such a finding would still hold in many instances today.

This information carries two important lessons. First of all, in our search for better capital-budgeting methodology, we should pay as much attention to calculating rates of return on human technical ability as we do to calculating rates of return on capital. That is, we cannot afford to overlook other constraining factors of production that may exist in addition to the problem of the supply of capital.

Second, we need to devise an informational system to help ensure that accepted projects are completely and rapidly integrated and that people are released from completed projects immediately so that other improvements and changes can be carried out.

INTERDEPENDENT PROJECTS

Neither Bierman nor Weston deals with the problem of interdependent investment projects. This is an area which needs more attention and one the practitioner needs to be aware of.

To illustrate this class of projects, suppose that the firm must decide how to provide transportation between two geographical points. Several forms of transport may be available — a variety of different trucks, a railroad, planes, and so forth. It is possible to use all the forms, but obviously, the rate of use of each would be different if all were installed from what it would be if only one were. These projects are not mutually exclusive (all could be selected) nor are they independent (the profitability of one is affected by the other). If one project is emphasized, the profit (or cost) characteristics of the others are changed. I suspect that this class of investments may form the largest and most important class of business investment projects. Rarely, for example, can a choice from related new product investments be made as if these projects were completely independent. Yet, our existing methodology and our recent search for improvements have largely ignored this kind of investment.

DETERMINING CASH FLOWS

In the outline of the process of capital budgeting given early in this discussion, I implicitly assumed that a cash-flow methodology, such as rate of return or net present value, was being used. As Bierman points out, there are other possible methods. But I agree with him that cash-flow methods have much to recommend them.

I think, however, it is necessary to point out that the "cash flow" as used in capital budgeting must be carefully distinguished from "cash flow" (especially cash flow per share) as used in corporate annual reports and in security analysis. In the latter context, cash flow really means "working capital" flow from operations. That is, the numerator for the calculation of cash flow per share is usually net profits after taxes plus depreciation and amortization.

If this same conceptual methodology is carried over into capital budgeting, large investments in working capital may be overlooked. Such a practice will inflate the return on investment. To illustrate, a large investment in inventory will use cash but will not affect or change working capital. However, if this expenditure is not included as part of the investment required by the project, the total investment will be understated and the rate of return or net present value will be overstated. Hence, in the measurement of cash flows for capital budgeting, it is highly important (as Bierman points out) that all changes in the *cash balance* associated with the project be carefully analyzed. The cash-flow method currently in favor with security analysts is too rough a measure to give good results in the selection of investment projects for a company.

ISOLATING THE INVESTMENT PROJECT

Another problem which must be discussed is one basic to the process of capital budgeting. We need to be constantly aware of it so that any adverse effects can be minimized.

We view capital budgeting as a process of dealing with individual and discrete capital investment projects. These projects are analyzed and selected or rejected as if the differential cash flows associated with each one can be isolated from the other cash flows associated with the firm in general. That is, we assume that the full effect of each project (or group of projects, if they are interdependent) on the total future cash flows of the firm can be determined. We then isolate each project from the rest of the operation of the firm and deal with it as an independent entity. This procedure is probably necessary in practice in order to simplify an extremely complex problem so it can be solved; however, it may, in many cases, oversimplify the situation, and we must be constantly aware of what's going on. Notice that the investment is isolated no matter which selection criterion is used — that is, whether we use payback or present value, we deal with projects isolated from total operations for purposes of comparison.

Bierman alludes to this situation in several places in his paper — let me call one to your attention. He mentions that a firm with a fixed facility may have excess capacity, and consequently a cash outflow may not be necessary for an investment project now under consideration. His example is a boiler. He also says that it can be shown that in most cases there is merit in including a cost of the use of this kind of fixed capacity. I suggest that the basic problem here is the practice of looking at and evaluating individual investment projects in isolation as if they were independent of other projects that may arise later. That is, the cost of using part of the fixed capacity of the firm now is that it will not be available for use later. Under conditions of certainty, one could look downstream, see what was coming along, and decide whether to use the excess capacity now or delay in favor of an opportunity that will arise next month or next year. The fact that investment decisions are made under conditions of uncertainty and the fact that we probably must look at projects individually will cause suboptimization from time to time. We must be aware of this problem and be prepared to accept the consequences in those instances where we cannot avoid it.

THE RELATION OF CASH FLOW AND COMPANY PROFITS

Finally, I should like to mention a problem which, so far as I know, has received little attention but which is very important to the management of the firm.

The capital-budgeting methodology discussed here and the one most widely accepted in the literature is based on discounted cash flow. However, a company may accept projects that return 25 per cent after taxes and find that earnings per share decline this year! That is, criteria for selection of investments geared to discounted cash flow may give optimal results for the firm in the long run, but the effect on short-run profits as they are reported to the financial community may not be to the liking of the management.

The reason for reported profits' not being perfectly correlated to discounted cash-flow procedures are many and complex. One simple thing to keep in mind is that any given project may have an acceptable time-adjusted rate of return but the cash inflows might not begin for three years. Hence, reported profits may be lower for a few years so far as this project is concerned. Furthermore, the total fixed costs for the firm are ignored (properly so) in selecting individual projects. When these fixed costs are included in the calculation of reported profits, the rate of return on accounting investment may be much different from what the management anticipated when it looked at the time-adjusted rate of return on individual projects.

This is a very difficult problem. However, the management of a company is typically as concerned with reported profits as with selecting new investments. The analyst of capital investment should at least give the management an indication of the effect of the capital budget on short-run reported profits, even though a discounted cash flow method based on differential cash flows for each investment project was used in selecting the budget. If the short-run effect on profits is not good, the management should at least be warned. Proper explanation of a decline in profits in the president's letter to stockholders would also aid the outside user of profit data.

SUMMARY AND CONCLUSION

In this discussion, I have probably raised more questions than I have answered. However, it is important to be aware of these problems and to understand their impact on capital budgeting tools. The tools of capital budgeting are not perfect, but they will be more effective in the hands of an informed management. Furthermore, these problems indicate a need and a direction for additional research. Current research has been focused mainly on problems of choosing criteria for selection and determining the cost of capital, and these problems are important; however, we should not ignore other directions of research that could pay handsome rewards.

Comments   **ROBERT W. JOHNSON**

IT IS worthwhile to observe that if these papers had been developed some years ago, it is unlikely that there would have been a section dealing with profits and corporate financial decisions. The two excellent papers that have been presented are indicative of the major role that financial management has assumed in contributing to the profitability of the firm. In the days of the senior Henry Ford, the production function was regarded as most essential in affecting profits; later on, the marketing function rose in importance as management became concerned about selling the end product of its highly efficient assembly lines. In earlier years, profits were regarded as originating mainly from production economies, shrewd marketing strategy, value buying, and the like. The financial manager was usually called in after decisions in the other functional areas had been made and told how much money was needed to support the profit-making activities of the firm.

Whereas he was formerly viewed as an unfortunately necessary part of overhead, the financial manager now makes a positive contribution to the profits of the firm, and our understanding of profits will be improved as we deepen our appreciation of the implications of this newly found role. When it is realized that decisions in all functional areas have financial implications, the financial manager is called upon to analyze plans originating in other areas in terms of their effect upon profitability and liquidity. Equally important, the financial manager now has a positive role in contributing to profits by exercising good management in raising funds and in allocating them appropriately within the firm. These key aspects of financial strategy are the subjects of Bierman's and Weston's papers.

It might be mentioned in passing that the new functions of finance have received recognition in our colleges and universities. Finance is rapidly ceasing to be a purely descriptive subject with encyclopedic listings of the different kinds of bonds and is becoming instead a course in financial strategy emphasizing the process of decision-making. This change has been brought about by a realization of the truth expressed by Weston that, as a result of the disequilibria and differential profitability opportunities in the real world, the opportunities for substantial contributions to profitability by good financial management are abundant.

If we examine the two papers together, it appears that the financial manager's contribution to profitability arises from two main activities: selection and timing. By selection, I mean that he selects from among various kinds and sources of funds and from among various proposals for capital expenditures. By timing, I mean that he tempers the process of selection by utilizing debt or equity funds to take advantage of transient moods of pessimism or optimism in the marketplace. Most investment decisions also involve timing — whether to replace a machine now or later, to expand now or later, or to refund debt now or later.

166

Weston has ably presented the variables that must be considered with respect to the selection process in determining the kinds and sources of funds to employ. It should be noted that both his model and the Modigliani-Miller model relate cost of capital to the degree of financial leverage, defined as debt over stock plus debt, in all cases taken at market value. Is this a suitable measure of the degree of leverage? Although it may be necessary to the Modigliani-Miller model because of its assumption of arbitrage, it does not appear to be necessary to Professor Weston's model. The debt-to-equity measure of leverage is essentially a balance-sheet approach, with the implicit assumption that this is the ratio viewed by the market as critical in determining the price-earnings ratio of the common stock. It seems more appropriate to determine the degree of leverage by calculating how much a change from any given level of income will affect the earnings on the common stock. This may be stated more precisely as "net income before interest and taxes divided by the net income after interest but before taxes." [1]

The difficulty with the debt-to-equity measure of leverage may be illustrated simply. Assume that two firms are in the same risk class, and that each firm employs $100 of twenty-year debt and $100 of equity at book value. However, Firm A was clever (or lucky) in timing its acquisition of debt, so that its debt carries a 4 per cent coupon, in contrast to the 5 per cent coupon on the debt of Firm B. If the market demands a yield of 5 per cent on the debt, the market value of the debt of A will be around $88 in contrast to $100 for the debt of B. (The debt of A may sell somewhat above $88 because of its better interest coverage.)

If operating incomes are $20 and $10, respectively, and if taxes are at a rate of 50 per cent, A will show earnings available for common stock of $8, whereas B will show earnings available of only $2.50. Moreover, the $8 earnings of A are likely to be valued more highly in the market because of their greater certainty and stability, in addition to possible expectations of future financial acumen or luck. For example, the common equity of A might sell at eleven times earnings, in contrast to six times earnings for Firm B. On the basis of these assumptions, it can be shown that the ratio of debt to debt plus equity at market value of Firms A and B will be 50 and 87 per cent respectively (the table on p. 169). A appears much more highly levered than B. The expected cost of the com-

[1] Pearson Hunt, "A Proposal for Precise Definitions of 'Trading on the Equity' and 'Leverage,'" *Journal of Finance*, XVI (September 1961), 383.

mon equity of A and B will be 9.1 per cent and 16.7 per cent respectively. The apparent extreme leverage is that found in the model proposed by Professor Weston and in the Modigliani-Miller model. If one uses Professor Hunt's measure of leverage, the results are less striking. By his definition, Firm B has a higher degree of financial leverage than Firm A, and the market recognizes this by demanding a yield of 16.7 per cent on equity in contrast to a yield of 9 per cent on the equity of the lower-levered firm.

Another aspect of selection that might be mentioned with reference to Weston's paper would be to add a note that selection does not end when a financial manager decides to finance his needs through a commercial bank or insurance company. Because of the wide variations in lending policies and positions, it pays a financial manager to shop among credit grantors to obtain the best offer. Such shopping would involve careful attention to requirements of compensating balances, cleanup periods, loan-to-security ratios, and willingness to innovate in lending policies.

Bierman has ably pointed out the deficiencies of the payback and the return-on-investment approaches to selection among investment proposals. A company using payback probably has little idea of the high hurdle it may be setting when it establishes a payback of two or three years. If the life of the investment is well over twice the payback period and if the annual cash flows from the project are relatively constant, a payback requirement of two years implies a rate of return of about 50 per cent after taxes, and a payback of three years about 33 per cent. By these standards, management may be rejecting investment proposals that it would be delighted to accept if it only realized the rate of return involved.

Although the relative merits of net present value and rate of return may not be as well established in favor of present value as Bierman suggests, there is not sufficient space to discuss this. A more crucial issue is the assumption in his analysis that capital rationing is not present. Examination of the patterns of the targets for cost of capital and return on capital noted by Professor Weston suggests that this assumption may rarely be met. For example, one wonders how many industrial concerns push capital expenditures down to a rate of return of 10 per cent. It seems likely that capital rationing often takes over before reaching the return-on-capital target. In this case independent investments become conflicting or mutually exclusive, and the process described for selection among mutually exclusive projects is no longer valid. Professor Bierman is clearly aware of this problem and that of dealing with risk. These are probably the two major unresolved issues of capital

Balance Sheet Leverage and Income Statement Leverage

Sources of Funds and Income Statement	Firm A[a]	Firm B[b]
Debt (20-year)	$100.00	$100.00
Equity	100.00	100.00
Total	$200.00	$200.00
Operating income	$ 20.00	$ 10.00
Interest	4.00	5.00
Income before taxes	$ 16.00	$ 5.00
Less taxes (50%)	8.00	2.50
Total income for common stock	$ 8.00	$ 2.50
Price-earnings ratio	11x	6x
Market value of equity (S)	$ 88.00	$ 15.00
Approximate market value of debt to yield 5% to maturity (D)	$ 88.00	$100.00
D/(D + S) at market	50%	87%
Expected yield on equity	9.1%	16.7%
Financial leverage[c]	1.25	2.0

[a] Debt carries coupon of 4 per cent.
[b] Debt carries coupon of 5 per cent.
[c] Defined as operating income divided by the quantity operating income minus interest.

budgeting today. My own view is that ultimately computers can be programed to select among investment proposals — giving proper regard to those that are mutually exclusive and to limitations desired by management to ration capital, to time future cash flows, to achieve a desirable risk pattern, and to give effect to major shifts in policy about the direction of the efforts of the firm.

Recognition in both papers of the importance of timing is to be applauded. It is a recognition of the real world of change and disequilibria that is essential to a meaningful theory of finance. However, this is an area in which we presently have inadequate knowledge. To build a model to judge the effect on the net present value of a business firm of a well-timed issue of bonds, we need to know more about the reactions of lenders and residual owners to changes and rates of change in capital structure, dividends, and earnings. Professors Weston and Bierman have both delineated the issues and made significant contributions to their solution. Each has pointed out that more remains to be done.

DANIEL M. HOLLAND

Risk and Rate of Return

EVERY trade has its perils. That of discussant is subject to the danger that the papers to be discussed may not be received before the meeting at which comments are to be made on them. Aware of this possibility, I started to build defenses by sketching out what I would say if I had no papers to discuss. Now I am in a dilemma, because although the papers by Professors Bierman and Weston were received well ahead of this conference, I had grown quite fond of my contingent presentation and was reluctant to cast it aside. So I have compromised. Rather than comment directly on these two papers — except to thank both Bierman and Weston for their excellent summaries and extension of the state of the arts — I shall spin out a little story of some research undertaken by Professor Paul Cootner and me, using a thread common to both papers under discussion. And the reason for this seeming obduracy is simply that the work we have done is relevant to business financing decisions and, more particularly, to points raised by Professors Bierman and Weston when they suggest the importance of uncertainty, utility, risk premia, and so forth. Professor Cootner and I have some results, as yet unpublished, that bear on these matters.

Our findings are by no means definitive — the most we can claim at this stage is that we have wrestled with some relevant questions and the results are interesting. Moreover, studies by some of our students

NOTE: I wish to acknowledge the help and advice of Professor Paul H. Cootner. In the preparation of this paper I have drawn freely on an as yet unpublished document prepared in collaboration with him for the American Telephone and Telegraph Company.

170

recently completed or currently under way tend in general to support the findings, although they show the need for much further study and thought. That our results are at present tentative, subject to many qualifications, and require deeper analysis, I will merely note but not amplify at this time. Specifically, our research sought to determine whether any relation exists between risk and the rates of return experienced by corporations. Thus, we were seeking to understand not profits so much as profit rates.

THEORETICAL BASIS OF THE MODELS

Looking at the rates of profit on capitalization earned by business firms, we see an enormous range of results. Some of this spread is undoubtedly due to random factors, but for a portion of it there may be a systematic explanation and it is with this possibility that we were concerned.

More particularly, we were interested in discovering whether a relation between rate of return and risk exists — i.e., whether risk premiums could be found in the spectrum of profit rates of business, or even more pointedly, whether that spread of results can be explained (realistically only in part, of course) by risk factors. It would seem that, given this interest, a sensible way to proceed would be to define rate of return and risk, specify the presumed relation between them, and test for its existence. But that would be premature, since before a start is made on such an effort, a basis for measurement must be established.

The basic precondition for measurement is an ordered world, that is, a world in which regularities exist and persist. Specifically, in the context of our interest in rates of return, in order to be able to go from what can in fact be observed to what theory suggests should motivate action — or, more particularly, in order to use observed rates of return as equivalent to expected rates of return — we need to assume that over a sufficiently long period of time managerial expectations are correct *on the average.* This is what John F. Muth has referred to as "rational expectations." [1] This assumption permits us to argue that, if the number of events is large enough, the distribution of actual outcomes of profit rates will closely approximate the distribution of expected outcomes. Thus, by observing what goes on in the "real" world, we could capture

[1] "Rational Expectations and the Theory of Price Movements," *Econometrica,* XXIX, No. 3 (July 1961), 315–335.

that seemingly ineffable item — what goes on in the mind of management. Having forged a link between observed data and the expectations that motivated the actions of management, we can then assert that it is possible to measure the relation between risk and rate of return in a meaningful way.

Rate of return or rate of profit is conceptually clear-cut; everyone uses it to mean much the same thing, and no formal definition is really necessary. Basically, it is a measure of the efficiency of capital use — that is, profit, that which is sought by the employment of capital in business is standardized for the amount of capital used in obtaining it. So we can consider rate of return to be the cents of profit (income) per dollar of capital, although it is generally more convenient to think of it as a percentage return. Admittedly, many alternatives exist for the definition of the numerator and denominator in calculating the rate, and endless debate is possible about which alternative to choose. To foreclose such debate, I note simply that in our study we used rather crude measures of each — the numerator, amount of return (income or profit), is defined as income after taxes but before interest payments and preferred dividends, whereas the denominator, capital at work, is measured by the firm's capitalization (equity plus long-term debt). Thus we sidestepped all problems connected with the most "appropriate" definition of income: the valuation of assets, factors making for incomparability of income among firms as of a given point in time, factors making for incomparability of income over time, and so forth. Clearly these are problems that deserve the most careful and thorough investigation. However, although we cannot, of course, be certain about this, we believe our findings would stand even with more carefully processed data.

"Rate of return" is analytically a clear-cut concept, but "risk" is something else again. Everyone would agree there is such a thing, but no consensus exists on a formal definition. However, there is more agreement than would at first appear on the basic element that gives a situation risky features and makes one situation riskier than another. It captures the essence of the problem to define as "risky" a situation in which more than one outcome is possible. To synonymize, risk is present whenever one is less than certain about the outcome of an action. Or, again, a risky situation is one characterized by a probability distribution of possible outcomes rather than a single, certain result. This latter view is most illuminating, for from it we infer that quantitative measures of the degree of risk or relative riskiness can be developed by reference to various features of the probability distribution of the possible outcomes of a given action.

But the ability to delineate risk, particularly in the context of a business investment, still does not get us all the way. How can risk be related to behavior? To see if the view of risk adopted has any operational value, we could ask whether the decision of management would be any different if, on a given outlay, 10 per cent could be earned with absolute certainty, from what it would be if yields of 8, 9, 10, 11, or 12 per cent were equally likely. Indeed, there are good reasons to believe that a businessman's response will differ in the two situations, even though the mean value is the same; to explain why we believe this, I must backtrack a bit.

Starting with your current income or wealth, ask yourself if you would be made as "happy" (I use this word for want of a better one) by an increase in it of 5 per cent as you would be made "unhappy" by a decrease in it of 5 per cent. Ask yourself also whether, considering only increases, a second increase of 5 per cent will bring just as much happiness as did the first. We believe most people will answer that in each of the hypothetical situations one of the alternatives will mean more happiness or satisfaction than the other, despite the equality of the mean monetary magnitudes associated with each. More specifically, we think it is reasonable to hold that most people would answer to the first question that a decrease of a given percentage would deprive them of more utility (the economist's word for happiness, satisfaction, or what you will) than an increase of the same percentage would add, and as to the second question, that most people most of the time would answer that the increase in utility associated with the second 5 per cent (of the original base) rise in income would not be so great as the increase associated with the first rise. The conclusion is that there is not a direct one to one correspondence between income or wealth and utility; utility does not change proportionally with money. In the typical case, the increases in utility (on its own scale, whatever it may be) are a declining function of income or wealth as the latter rise or, conversely, an increasing function as income or wealth falls.

All this is background to my earlier question, which I repeat. Would

173

management look differently on the two following situations, each requiring the same outlay: in one the rate of return would be 10 per cent for certain, whereas in the other it could be 8, 9, 10, 11, or 12 per cent all with equal likelihood? Now it is understandable why we thought most people would probably see a difference between the two situations, for it is consistent with the observed behavior of economizers, and with introspection too, to hold that it is utility, not income, that people seek to maximize. From this, if we assume marginal utility declines, we can see why the situation with a certain 10 per cent offers a better opportunity than does the situation with a mean value of 10 per cent and the possibility of earning either more or less. In particular, the increase in utility associated with the outcome of either the 11 or 12 per cent would not be so great as the decline thereof should the return of 8 or 9 per cent eventuate.

Businessmen, then, are motivated by the return they think they can earn on their assets; the relevant expected value for their decisions is not the possible monetary returns weighted by the probability of their occurrence, but the possible monetary returns weighted by both their utility and the probability of their occurrence. In a risky situation, management seeks to maximize expected utility, not expected money income, and the key to analyzing businessmen's (or any other economizing agent's) reaction to risk is the differential utility associated with additional amounts of income.

Earlier I noted that a risky situation is one characterized by a probability distribution of outcomes rather than a single, certain result. Now, in the light of the discussion of utility, I can suggest that, other things equal, the degree of risk will be determined by the dispersion of this probability distribution. (Other features of the probability distribution, for example, skewness, may also be important here, but we concentrated on dispersion.) It is clear that of two investment opportunities — both with a mean rate of return of 10 per cent and both requiring the same outlay — that which had a .9 chance of 10 per cent and .1 chance of 9 or 11 per cent would be preferred to that which promised 8, 9, 10, 11, or 12 per cent with equal probability. This statement, in common with all such about what people prefer or like, rests on assumptions about taste. Specifically, for reasons just developed, businessmen are assumed to like return and dislike risk. We assumed that investors and management in general are "risk averters." [2] Operationally, this has the following consequences: If management is willing to pay the same price for two investment opportunities, X and Y, and X has a wider dispersion of outcomes (a greater risk) than Y, then X's expected return must be greater than Y's. Or, again, if X is preferred to Y and both have the same expected return, then X's dispersion of outcomes must be smaller than Y's. In other words, the decisions of management trade off between risk and return.

The discussion up to this point has been directed particularly to two items — the probability distribution of the outcomes and the marginal utility of income. Neither, of course, is easy to get at. As far as the latter goes, we assume (reasonably, we believe) that the general attitudes of investors in physical assets (or financial assets also, for that matter, although this was not our concern) can be characterized by declining marginal utility and risk aversion. As for risk itself, we have chosen as a first approximation to direct our attention to a reasonable measure of dispersion — the standard deviation of the distribution of returns — although we recognize the importance of other measures of dispersion and other features of the probability distribution and did do, in both connections, some experimenting that I shall not report here.

So much for a brief summary of the theoretical basis of our study. Before turning to the particular models specified and tested, I note that our sample consisted of 315 large manufacturing and retailing firms classified in 39 industrial groups, and our tests used data on these firms for the period 1946–1960.

INDUSTRY RATE OF RETURN AS A FUNCTION OF DISPERSION WITHIN THE INDUSTRY OF RATES OF RETURN

The first attempt to quantify the relation between risk and rate of return was directed to industrial rates of return — i.e., averages of the profit rates of firms in the industry. We considered, for reasons explained above, that the dispersion of rates of return for individual companies

[2] No slur, of course, is intended here. It is the business of management to assume risk, and I do not mean to suggest that management shirks its duty. To be a risk averter is, other things equal, to prefer less risk to more risk and, therefore, to accept greater risk only if there is the prospect of a higher rate of return. To say that businessmen are risk averters is to say no more or less than that it would generally be considered poor business practice to choose investment B rather than investment A if both cost the same and have the same expected return, but B was riskier than A.

around the average rate of return of the industry to which they belong is a meaningful indicator of the riskiness of a commitment of resources to that industry. Since the standard deviation (a widely used measure of dispersion) of such rates of return is an index of the likelihood that an investor would fare differently from the industry average, we should expect, if executives were risk averters, that industries with high standard deviations would require high average rates of return to attract investment. We specified, therefore, a simple linear model: $I = aX_1 + b$ where I is the average industry rate of return on capitalization, X_1 is the standard deviation of company rates of return around the unweighted [3] industry average, and b is a constant.

The test of this model for 39 industries over the period 1946–1960 indicated a statistically significant relation between rate of return and the measure of risk used:

$$I = .935X_1 + 8.18 \quad [4]$$
$$(.230)$$

Since the coefficient of X_1, the risk variable, is positive, the equation says that the higher the risk, the higher the predicted industry rate of return. It suggests that a 1 per cent increase in risk is associated with close to a 1 per cent increase in industry rate of return. The correlation (a measure of the strength of the association) between I and X_1 is .55 and is statistically significant. A value of .55 means that about 30 per cent ($.55 \times .55$) of the variability of industry rate of return is explained by the dispersion of company rates of return around the industry average. This is an accomplishment, but it of course falls far short of explaining a major portion of the differences in rates of return among industries. To revert to the estimated relation (the regression line), the constant term 8.18 implies that an industry without any risk of the kind measured by X_1 would have an 8.18 per cent return on its capitalization. That the "riskless" rate of return in this context is so high serves merely to emphasize that the relation accounts for only one kind of

[3] Later tested with weighted averages and found to have no significant effect on our findings.

[4] The numbers in parentheses are the standard errors of the estimated values of the regression coefficients and are used to determine whether an estimated value is significant. As a general rule, if the estimate is ± 2.6 times its standard error, there is only one chance in one hundred that the true value is zero. It is a convention to consider estimated values that are at least this much greater than their standard error as indicating that the coefficient is significant — i.e., its true value is not zero. By this yardstick all the coefficients of our regression equations are significant.

risk and for only 30 per cent of the variability in I. As we shall see in the company rates of return model, eliminating other kinds of risk reduces the "risk-free" rate of return.

In addition to variations in industry rates of return, we sought to explain differences among company rates of return by enlarging the sample from 39 observations for industries to 315 for companies. It is important to point this up, because it obviously means that for companies there is a lot more to explain. Here we tried models of the form $Y = a_1 X_1 + c$ where Y is the average rate of return on capitalization for a company for the postwar period 1946–1960, the X_1 are various measures of dispersion, and c is a constant.

After much experimentation it turned out that as good an explanation as any was afforded by a two-variable regression:

$$Y = .788X_1 + .944X_2 + 5.31$$
$$(.157) \quad (.115)$$

where X_1 is the standard deviation of the rates of return of the company over the postwar period around the mean of the industry to which the company belongs for that same period, and X_2 is the standard deviation of the annual rates of return for the company around the postwar average. The multiple correlation coefficient, statistically significant, is .502. Since this regression involves two explanatory variables, it may be informative to sift out their relative importance in explaining company rate of return. The second variable, X_2, has a simple correlation with Y of .437 and hence is more useful than X_1 in explaining company rate of return. That is to say, X_2 alone explains 19 per cent of the variation in Y, whereas adding X_1 to X_2 in the regression results in an additional 6 per cent being accounted for.

One may ask at this point, What progress has been made, if any? In the industry regression which used only one explanatory variable, R was .55; now, with two explanatory variables, R is .50. But, indeed, these company rate of return results are more noteworthy statistically, for the explanation applies to 315 companies, not 39 industries, and hence the regression (the presumed functional relation between risk and rate of return) has borne a much greater statistical burden. And they are more credible also because we would expect that there would exist risk variables related to the company per se as well as risk variables associated with the industry to which the company belongs.

Recalling the industry regression, we can learn from the company regression that if X_2 is held constant and X_1 increases by 1 per cent, then Y will increase by only .788 per cent instead of the .955 per cent associated with it when X_2 was free to vary. Similarly, if X_1 were held constant and X_2 increased by 1 per cent, Y would increase by .94 per cent. The other major change resulting from taking two kinds of risk into account is that the predicted "risk-free" rate of return on long-term investment (equity plus long-term debt was the denominator in computing rate of return) falls from 8.2 to 5.3 per cent. And this is a heartening change, for, considering the relative illiquidity of industrial plant and equipment (and we have not measured the risk of illiquidity) compared with, say, government bonds, the 5.3 per cent is a reasonable figure. And it is of course to be expected that a relation that purports to adjust for two kinds of risk will show a lower "risk-free" rate of return than a regression that incorporates only one kind of risk.

So much for our results. What do we make of them? The occasion permits only the briefest of summaries and a warning. We think the results enable us to say that risk premia are in fact substantiated by the pattern of corporate rates of return, and that we are proceeding in a sensible and fruitful way in seeking to explain them. The riskier the industry or firm the higher its profit rate — yet at best this is a tentative finding. Much remains to be refined and investigated in depth. Our most important conclusion, then, is an invitation to other investigators to join in research in this area. We believe it will pay off.

PROFITS AND NATIONAL
ECONOMIC POLICY ✦ ✦ ✦

Editors' Introduction

THE annual Economic Report of the President to the Congress is awaited by the citizens of the United States as an important document, and they have accorded the President's Council of Economic Advisers a place of importance in the national life. The Employment Act of 1946, which provides for the message, is a declaration of national purpose and is a recognition of federal responsibility for the promotion of "maximum employment, production, and purchasing power." As can be surmised, an economy with full employment would, among other attributes, reward enterprise with profit. Just how profits are viewed in the shaping of national economic policy is the subject of Walter Heller's paper. The original paper, written when he was chairman of the Council of Economic Advisers, has been brought up to 1966 by Dr. Heller. The revised paper thus provides perspective for the influences of Vietnam, a look into the future, and a fitting conclusion to these papers on profits.

Dr. Heller draws a contrast between profits in business as an end of policy and profits in government as a means of policy. In national economic policy, profits have a role derived essentially from other policies. For improvement in profits and profit rates, Dr. Heller underscores two requirements: a return to full employment and the maintenance of good management by private decision makers.

The Role of Profits in National Economic Policy

IN HIS paper, Richard Holton said he need not preach the virtues of profits to *this* congregation — that the brethren are already saved. But here I am assuming that the congregation is asking whether the *preacher* — in this case, the government — is saved. At the end of this sermon, I hope that the congregation will have a reasonably reliable answer — that you will know whether the Administration is in league with the angels or the devils of your choice.

The role of profits in national economic policy is essentially a derived one — derived from policies for growth, for full employment, for price stability, for balance-of-payments equilibrium, for equality of economic opportunity.

For private business, profits are the end — not the only end, but the *living* end — of policy. But for government, profits are primarily a means: They enter growth policy as a goad to private risk-taking and innovation, as a source of funds for expansion, and as a guide to efficient resource flow. They enter balance-of-payment policy as an incentive to the productivity advances that bring lower costs and a stronger competitive position; they enter too as a source of the higher domestic rates of return that keep American capital at home. They enter price policy both indirectly as a stimulant to cost-cutting modernization and directly as a reflector of rapid productivity gains that permit price reductions. They enter full-employment policy, partly as an ingredient (as a contributor to the investment component of full-employment demand) but mainly as the by-product of success in such policy. They enter distributional policy, especially through taxation, as a focus of measures to strengthen small business relative to large, or strengthen one distributive share relative to another.

So profits are sometimes an *instrument* of national economic policy, sometimes a *result*, sometimes a *guide*, sometimes a *target*. And the specific role of profits in policy at any given time will inevitably respond to the changing national priorities assigned to various economic objectives in the light of changing economic circumstance. The day has long since passed when governmental attitudes or policy on profits can be judged — or determined — in terms of gross desires to be benign or beastly to business, to deify or denigrate profits as such. Understanding the role of profits requires digging deeper — down to the bedrock of economic fact, philosophy, and priorities.

Therefore let me examine the changed demands on economic policy that have grown out of our deficits in the balance of payments externally and our deficits in demand internally — out of our need to reconcile policies for external equilibrium with policies for internal full employment and faster growth. What role has emerged for profits out of this process? How has this role been reflected in related profits and cash flow? And finally, what is the role of future profits policy in sustained and balanced economic expansion?

In exploring whether the winds of change are blowing warm zephyrs or wintry blasts in the direction of profits, we should not lose sight of the abiding role assigned to profits in both classical and Keynesian economics. No one has expressed this role with greater wisdom, wit, and brevity than Kenneth Boulding:

The classical justification for a profits system is that, on the whole, profits are made by being serviceable. Businesses can only thrive by selling people things that they want at prices which they can afford and which will enable the business to attract the resources necessary. This is less romantic than selling people what you think is good for them, like glory, death, progress and salvation, but it at least exhibits a decent humility. Serviceable enterprises can attract both capital and labor; what is serviceable will be profitable, and what is profitable will be done.

And he offers some amusing *obiter dicta*:

Curiously, perhaps the greatest virtue of profit, as a goal of organizational policy and as a measure of success, is its abstractness — the very quality that has brought it most into disrepute with the romantics who yearn (and I confess to a small yearn along with them) for a world in which everything is done for love . . . if we cannot do everything for

183

love, there is at least a certain innocence about doing things for money. Making money may not be a heroic, romantic, or self-sacrificing occupation (though it may sometimes be so) but it at least avoids the particular morass of corruption into which mankind is apt to slip when it makes utopias.[1]

THE RISING EMPHASIS ON INVESTMENT

Profits, then, always constitute a worthy — and sometimes even a witty — subject for businessmen and economists to discuss. But what makes this discussion now exceptionally timely is the rising concern over profits and investment on the part of groups both here and abroad who have traditionally not been particular partisans of profits. I refer, for example, to the Labour Party in Britain, to many center or left-of-center parties in Western Europe, and to "liberal" Democrats in this country. This heightened concern grows chiefly out of the commitment to faster economic growth and the need to strengthen international competitive positions.

This country has become more investment-minded, first, because it has become more growth-minded and because it recognizes the heavy dependence of an economy's productivity growth on its rate of capital formation. Certainly, none of us subscribes to an oversimplified theory of economic growth that makes productivity growth dependent wholly on investment trends. Plainly, the productivity outcome is also affected by a great variety of other influences, such as the quality of labor, of capital, and of management. Plainly, too, the investments that yield the sought-for advances in productivity include not only private investment but many kinds of public investment as well, include not only outlays for plant and equipment but investments in human brainpower and in research and development, and exclude some kinds of private investment (in today's circumstances, for example, American private investment overseas).

But, granting all of this, there is still a powerful presumptive relation between the portion of national output that, over a period of years, is channeled into business fixed investment and the trend rate at which output per man hour rises. Broadly construed, this has been our experience in this country. And it is what economic analysis tells us. Increased investment raises the productivity of labor by endowing

[1] "A Look at the Corporation," *The Lamp*, 1957 (75th anniversary volume of Jersey Standard), pp. 6–7.

the worker with more and better tools. Technical progress does not float down on the productive process like a spirit, endowing old machinery with new life. Usually, the innovations of engineers and analysts must be embodied in new capital goods before they can move from the drawing board into the shop.

Second, we have become productivity-minded — and therefore investment-minded — because of the new demands of *balance-of-payments policy*. During the years after 1957, our international economic flanks became exposed.

Before 1957, the world hunger for dollars made our balance-of-payments deficits a welcome source of world liquidity. The United States could and did keep its international door and its pocketbook open and still pursue domestic goals of growth and full employment as if it were a closed economy. But in 1957–1958 the major world currencies became freely convertible, the dollar shortage began to turn into a dollar glut, and gold began to flow out faster. The economy became, in fact, open.

At the same time, growth slowed down and stubborn unemployment developed. The search for policies to reconcile the expansionary requirements of internal economic policy with the restrictive requirements of external policy led directly to greater emphasis on stepping up of productivity. Faster increases in productivity, in reduction of costs per unit of output, serve to strengthen our competitive position in world markets, to improve the returns on domestic relative to overseas investments, thus stemming long-term capital outflows, and to permit domestic expansion to proceed within a framework of price stability as rapid productivity advances satisfy appetites for higher wages and profits without higher prices.

Yet, side by side with the growing consensus on the importance of investment for productivity in recent years, we had a falling rate of investment in relation to GNP. After 1956, we failed to maintain the high rates of investment in plant and equipment of the first postwar decade, and they have only recently returned to those earlier levels.

During the postwar period *as a whole*, fixed investment of business as a share of GNP has been substantially higher than during the 1930's and World War II (as a whole). And in good part for this reason, productivity gains have been faster since the war. But after 1957, when the economy developed a persistent slack in both demand and employment, slack also appeared in the ratio of fixed investment of business to

GNP. The ratio fell from an average of 10.8 per cent for the years 1947–1957 to an average of 9 per cent. Only in 1965 and 1966 has it come back to levels of 10.5 per cent. It may reach 11 per cent by 1967.

Somewhat surprisingly, and counter to past trend experience, the rate of growth in output per man hour did not sag along with investment after 1957. Though one cannot yet be sure, this experience suggests that, first, the rate of productivity growth does indeed depend on many factors in addition to the rate of capital accumulation — perhaps the quality of new capital, or of labor or management, has been improving faster in recent years, and second, we have not been taking full advantage of these other contributions to economic growth; if we had been able to couple them with a sustained high rate of private capital formation — and high aggregate demand — the productivity experience would have been even more impressive.

The combination of circumstances just reviewed has unmistakably raised the long-run priority assigned to public efforts to stimulate higher private investment (though there may be periods — as in 1966, under pressures of Vietnam — when the increased demand-pull effect of capital spending on short-run inflationary pressures may temporarily outweigh its benign long-run effects in reducing cost-push pressures). And these efforts have, inevitably, highlighted measures that increase the profitability of private capital investment.

POLICY MEASURES AFFECTING PROFITS

Tax stimulants to investment have played the key role in translating the new emphasis in policy into action. The first phase of the coordinated program, in 1962, raised annual corporate cash flow after taxes by nearly $2.5 billion through more liberal depreciation and a special tax credit for domestic plant and equipment outlays. The corporate tax provisions of the revenue act of 1964 reduce corporate tax liabilities by another $2.5 billion and broaden the investment tax credit.

But the cash-flow benefits of these tax changes are not the only, or even the major, contribution they make to encourage investment. Their incentive effects, operating through the prospective rate of return on new investment, are even more striking. For example, the Department of the Treasury has estimated that for a typical piece of equipment with a ten-year service life and 100 per cent equity financing, the after-tax rate of return was raised some 35 per cent as a result of the tax changes of 1962 and 1964. Such an improvement in return will stimulate more investment in American enterprise by Americans and thus keep some capital home that might have been tempted to go abroad. It may also attract some foreign capital into American use.

Monetary policy has been carefully coordinated with tax policy in a two-pronged attack on our domestic and balance-of-payments problems. Close Treasury-Federal Reserve cooperation — using such tools as sales of short-term bills and purchases of long-term government securities — has played an important role in twisting the interest rate structure: it has pushed up the rates on short-term, fluid funds that might otherwise readily run out of the country in response to higher rates abroad — and has thus cut down our balance-of-payments deficit. At the same time, it has until recently held down the cost of funds that go into long-term investment in housing, public capital, plant and equipment — and has thus stimulated productivity growth and facilitated domestic expansion.

In speaking of measures designed to encourage investment directly, let me mention again our emphasis on investment in human capital, as well as physical investment. Such measures as the Manpower Development and Training Act of 1962, the Higher Education Facilities Construction Act of 1963, and the Economic Opportunity Act of 1964 (the poverty bill) illustrate the broad sweep of the Administration's program in this area.

In this review of policies about profits, we should remind ourselves that investment in human capital, though a desirable goal in itself, finds its ultimate *productive* justification in the fact that a more skilled and knowledgeable labor force is more profitable to employ.

The last item on my list of the Administration's policies to promote investment — namely, measures to expand consumer markets — is in some ways the most important. To provide the strongest possible incentive to capital investment requires strong markets — full use of existing resources.

We need not go beyond our natural desire to minimize waste and want and to lead the Free World to justify vigorous full-employment policies. But full profits are an important by-product of full employment of our resources.

The sensitivity of the profits share in output to changes in use of resources is clearly shown in Figure 1. When total economic performance is deficient, profits are deficient. The strongest single boost to profits and to anticipations of profit — and therefore to investment — that any government can provide comes from a commitment to a full-employment, full-utilization policy without inflation. That commitment on the part of the United States government, first expressed in the Employment Act of 1946, was renewed and sharpened by the revenue act of 1964.

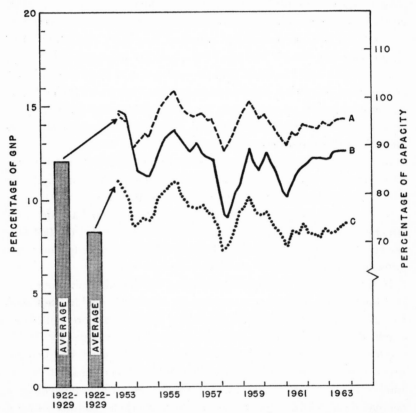

Figure 1. Capacity utilization and corporate profits. Line A represents corporate cash flow as a percentage of GNP (left scale) — that is, corporate profits (before taxes) and inventory valuation adjustment plus capital consumption allowances as a percentage of GNP; B, manufacturing capacity utilization (right scale); and C, corporate profits as a percentage of GNP (left scale) — that is, corporate profits (before taxes) and inventory valuation adjustment as a percentage of GNP. (Data from Department of Commerce and Federal Reserve Board. Data have subsequently been revised, but effect on this chart is insignificant.)

188

Profits and National Economic Policy

The importance of full utilization of resources is graphically illustrated in the successive upward revisions of 1964 investment plans by business as passage of the tax bill became increasingly certain. The McGraw-Hill fall survey in 1963 showed an anticipated increase of only 4 per cent in total plant and equipment expenditures for 1964 over 1963 levels. A special January 1964 survey, again by McGraw-Hill, showed the figure rising to 9 per cent, and not all of this increase could be explained by the usual understatement in the fall survey. The Department of Commerce–Securities Exchange Commission (Commerce–SEC) survey in February showed an anticipated increase of 10 per cent. The McGraw-Hill survey made after the tax cut was enacted and published in April 1964 showed a rise of 12 per cent.

The tax bill started the economy on its way back to full employment and also signaled the end of the slack season for investment.

In appraising the record of measures to improve profits and productivity, my paper has, by design, concentrated on public policies. But the interplay of public and private policies is so close that it would be a serious omission to overlook the role that the quality of private management has played in this expansion.

We have had a very tightly managed business expansion since 1961. I shall not turn sociologist and attempt to explain the changes wrought. But the unmistakable fact is that these changes have been there: Managers have been more alert, economizing, and orderly in their control of *inventories*. They have been judicious but also forehanded in their *fixed investment* decisions, searching for cost-saving innovations and investments and keeping their capacities advancing a step — but not five or ten steps — ahead of sales. As a result, *new orders* have maintained a balanced relation to production. And in recent months, when the expansion has accelerated, there has been little bunching of unfilled orders and remarkably few signs of incipient bottlenecks. Managers, not spasmodically but characteristically, have been *cost-conscious* in this expansion, making their buying and hiring decisions with a sharp pencil. The comparative stability of prices — even in markets where there is a good deal of discretion in pricing decisions — suggests that many managers have been *setting prices with an eye to volume* and to longer-run competitive considerations. The over-all orderliness of the expansion also has minimized the generation of pressures that would have made for inflation in commodity markets. And management and labor jointly have agreed on wage increases that, on the average, have hewed close to the line of national productivity gains.

One result of the good management that has characterized the expansion has of course been a better showing than otherwise would have been made on the productivity front. But another — indeed, almost a mirrored — result has been a better showing for profits than would otherwise have been possible.

IMPACTS ON PROFITS AND CASH FLOW

Let us look briefly now at the impact that these private and public policies have had on profit performance in the 1961–1966 expansion. Richard Holton's paper emphasizes many of the difficulties and many of the needed adjustments in making comparisons of profits in different periods. And he draws the major lessons from the data. I need only add a few footnotes.

Table 1. Corporate Profits over Five Postwar Expansions (in billions of dollars, in current prices)[a]

| Period of Expansion | Quarters of Expansion | Before Taxes and Inventory Valuation Adjustment | | After Taxes | |
		Quarterly Average	Total	Quarterly Average	Total
1946 I–1948 IV	12	26.0	77.9	19.5	58.4
1949 III–1953 II ...	16	39.2	156.7	21.5	86.0
1954 III–1957 III ..	13	45.5	148.0	26.2	85.0
1958 II–1960 II	9	48.8	109.7	26.6	59.9
1961 II–1966 I	20	62.0	310.0	35.8	178.8

SOURCE: Data from Department of Commerce.

[a]Seasonally adjusted annual rates. Data exclude profits originating in the rest of the world.

First, Table 1 compares cumulative corporate profits before taxes in the current expansion with those in previous postwar expansions. During the twenty quarters ending in the first quarter of 1966, total profits were $310.0 billion. This is more than double the total profits earned in the thirteen quarters of the 1954–1957 expansion and nearly double the profits earned in the sixteen quarters of the expansion spanning the Korean war. The $62 billion average rate of profits since the second quarter of 1961 is 30 per cent better than the previous high average in the 1958–1960 expansion. The after-tax profit comparisons are, of course, even more favorable on each count.

Second, Table 2 points up the sustained growth of profits in this expansion in contrast to the more characteristic spurt, then trailing off, of profits in 1954–1956 and 1958–1960. It also highlights the dramatic

Table 2. Corporate Profits and Capital Consumption Allowances
(in billions of dollars, in current prices)[a]

| Year | Corporate Profits | | Corporate Capital Consumption Allowances | Corporate Profits after Taxes *plus* Capital Consumption Allowances |
	Before Taxes *and* Inventory Valuation Adjustment	After Taxes		
1947	25.6	20.2	5.8	26.0
1948	33.0	22.7	7.0	29.7
1949	30.8	18.5	7.9	26.5
1950	37.7	24.9	8.8	33.7
1951	42.7	21.6	10.3	31.8
1952	39.9	19.6	11.5	31.0
1953	39.6	20.4	13.2	33.5
1954	38.0	20.6	15.0	35.5
1955	46.9	27.0	17.4	44.4
1956	46.1	27.2	18.9	46.1
1957	45.6	26.0	20.8	46.8
1958	41.1	22.3	22.0	44.3
1959	51.7	28.5	23.5	52.0
1960	49.9	26.7	24.9	51.6
1961	50.3	27.2	26.2	53.5
1962	55.7	31.2	30.1	61.3
1963	58.1	32.6	32.0	64.5
1964	64.5	37.2	34.0	71.2
1965	73.1	44.5	36.1	80.5

SOURCE: Data from Department of Commerce.
[a]Data exclude profits originating in the rest of the world.

rise in depreciation allowances, which reflects both the progressive liberalizing of depreciation allowances for tax purposes, especially in 1954 and 1962, and the catching up of depreciation allowances with higher postwar levels of replacement costs. Capital consumption allowances were only $8.8 billion in 1950. By 1961 they had risen nearly threefold, and in 1962 alone they jumped $4 billion.

During the late 1940's and early 1950's, businessmen often complained that profits were overstated because of too low depreciation. The intervening price trends, together with the elimination of older items from the capital stock, have substantially eased this problem. In addition, under the benign influence of favorable tax provisions — especially the 1962 guidelines — substantial revenues formerly labeled "profits" are now labeled "depreciation allowances."

For many purposes, therefore, long-term comparisons of earnings can best be made on the basis of cash flow — profits after taxes plus depreciation. On this basis, 1965 was indeed a "big" year compared with earlier postwar years: cash flow reached $80.5 billion for the year and an annual rate of $83 billion for the fourth quarter — almost two and a half times the 1950 rate and almost twice as high as the 1955 rate.

Some of the nominal gains have of course been offset by price increases. But even after cash flow is deflated by the index of new plant and equipment prices to get a measure of the "capital goods purchasing power" of the accruals to corporations, deflated cash flow for the year 1965 was about 50 per cent higher than in the earlier peak profit years of 1955 and 1959.

THE PRESENT CHALLENGE

The first element of this profits story was the development of the economic conditions and convictions that led to a consensus on the need for faster productivity growth and, therefore, for measures to stimulate investment through adequate profit incentives. Second, we have considered the public policies adopted for this purpose, together with private managerial policies contributing to profitable expansion. Third, we have looked briefly at the reflection of these policies in the actual profits record of the 1961–1966 expansion.

That reflection is encouraging. There have been good profits. Their growth has been unusually well sustained. And up until very recently, they have not been associated with price increases or with attempts to inflate margins. Profits increases will be slowing now that capacity is starting to limit the rate of economic expansion and a larger fraction of subsequent output gains is likely to accrue to labor. The present challenge is to avoid inflation in the environment by avoiding the battle over shares that would unleash it. Or, to put it in terms of profits, the challenge is to keep profits advancing out of higher productivity, not at the expense of healthy (i.e., productivity-bounded) wage growth and price stability.

Profits and National Economic Policy

So the end of this particular story has yet to be written. If it is to be thoroughly happy, two requirements must be met: First, we must keep demand at full-employment, full-capacity levels. At this stage, nothing else — recall the relation between profits and utilization rates in Figure 1 — is so clearly designed to bolster profits, simultaneously with employment, personal income, and government revenues. And nothing else, experience also tells us, is so clearly calculated to call forth a sustainably higher rate of investment. It is only when there is the pull of a full-employment market on investment that we can expect to get full mileage out of the boosters to incentives and cash flow supplied by the 1962–1964 corporate tax changes. And we must not permit inflationary pressures — whether caused by Vietnam, as in 1966, or by other sources in later years — to distort and unbalance our expansion and thereby force the nation to slam on its economic brakes.

This is where the second requirement enters, the critical need for private decision makers to maintain the same good management, cost consciousness, sense of order and balance, and restraint in wage negotiations and price-making that have been the hallmarks of the expansion thus far. If we were now to lose these qualities — if market power were used to obtain excessive profit margins or excessive wage increases at the expense of consumers, if the price-wage spiral is reactivated — then we would run the risks of losing our hard-won gains on the balance-of-payments front, of touching off new conflicts between our external and domestic economic objectives and — within the domestic context — between our goals of growth and of stability, and of shortening the life expectancy of this old but still lean and vital expansion.

Apart from the economic turbulence associated with Vietnam, I do not expect such an unpleasant end to the profits story of the 1960's. For with the public policies that now have been put in place, with a continuation of constructive private policies, and with exercise of both public and private responsibility, our hopeful prospect in the period beyond Vietnam can be one of sustained and growing prosperity — one that will generate, among other good things, sustained and growing profits

INDEX + + +

Index

Abramovitz, Moses, 104n
Accounting: definition of income, 63–72; principles of, 71, 73; conservatism of, 73, 73–74; terminology of, 74; data in, 80, 90, 164–165
AFL-CIO, 35
Alchian, Armen, 104n
Alchian-Kessel theory, 137
Alexander, Sidney S., 63, 63n
Analysts Handbook, 44–45
Ando, Albert, 64, 64n
Andrews, Victor, 149n
Arbitrage, 135–136, 167
Assortment: problem of, 118

Balance of payments, 185, 193
Barges, Alexander, 135n
Baty, Gordon, 150n
Bauman, Jacqueline, 22, 46n
Baxter, W. T., 63n
Bell, Philip W., 70n, 91, 110n, 115n
Benishay, Haskell, 145n
Bierman, Harold, Jr., 62, 160, 163, 164, 166–169 *passim*, 170
Boddy, Francis M., 161
Bodenhorn, Diran, 62, 93, 99n, 104n, 113n
Boulding, Kenneth: on profits, 183–184
Brown, Murray, 23, 23n
Budget, United States Bureau of the, 43
Business Cycle Developments, 47, 55
Business Economics, Office of, 41, 46
Butters, J. Keith, 39n

Capacity: 10, 34; and capital budgeting, 164
Capital, costs of: 128–130, 134–159, 160,

168; as a cutoff rate, 132; problems of measuring, 141–147
"Capital and Rates of Return in Manufacturing Industries" (Stigler), 33
Capital budgeting, 129, 134, 160–165, 168
Capital consumption allowances, 23
Capitalization: return on, 171
Cash balance: in capital budgeting, 163
Cash flow: 99–101, 160, 164–165, 186, 192; effect of on investment, 10; distribution of, 29–32, 32–33; in performance evaluation, 64; concept of profit, 98–116; in capital budgeting, 162–163; in security analysis, 163
Childs, John F., 144, 144n
Clark, J. B., 3
Commerce, United States Department of, 41, 42, 43, 44, 45, 46, 47, 49, 51, 52, 55, 57, 189
Conservatism: in accounting, 78–79, 121
Cootner, Paul H., 62, 87, 170
Corporation Records, 44
Costs: effects of on profits, 54, 70; calculating, 69, 70–71
Coupon rates, 141
Cyert, Richard M., 67n

Davidson, Sidney, 63n
Dean, Joel, 99n
Debtor-creditor: in Alchian-Kessel theory, 137; firms' status as, 144, 146
Demand: effect of on profits, 53–54; aggregate, 186
Depreciation: 31–32, 109–112; effect of on profit, 19–20, 51–52; allowances for, 35–36, 186, 191–192

197